Tortilla Diaries

A year spent travelling solo through Latin America

Marina Fusella

To all the people I met along the way of this mad journey, (without you this book wouldn't be the same) and of course, to my family.

TORTILLA DIARIES

28/01/21

The beginning of my trip felt like starting a Monopoly game straight from prison. I was due to fly from London to Guatemala, but a few weeks prior to my departure, due to the Delta variant of Covid 19, the Guatemalan government closed its borders to people that have been in the UK 14 days before arrival. Under suggestion of a friend, my new plan was to fly home to Italy, stay there for 14 days, then fly to Spain hoping to join my original flight to Guatemala.

So, I have been spending the last two weeks in self-isolation at my cousin's flat, overlooking the bay of Naples – Moody cobalt grey, stormy and bright blue skies mirrored themselves in the sea randomly, as I found myself in Naples precisely in the short winter, that this year, happens to be right now. At times the sky has been loaded with fat dollops of rain, coming down hard, whilst snow covers the top of Vesuvius.

Finally, this morning, after days of uncertainty and stress checking governments websites for latest coronavirus rules, hoping that no more borders would shut in front of me, I left Naples by coach.

I have my negative Covid test and I am attempting to escape all the way to Guatemala, crossing borders: Naples, Rome, Madrid, Panama and Guatemala City.

At Rome airport I collect all my tickets. I now know that I will be definitely boarding the plane! I can finally breathe and relax.

I try to sleep on the long flight with some success.

At Tocumen Airport, Panama, all passengers must fill in a health declaration form. I chat to another traveller, Raul, who borrows my phone charger, and we talk about where I shall visit. He also helps me with my form, before we both help two other passengers. I am pleasantly surprised as I understand a lot of what is being said and I manage to communicate in very basic Spanish.

35 hours later I finally get to Guatemala City and opt for a shuttle to Antigua after going through customs without hassle. However, it is a bit scary; two sniffer dogs come to sniff me up. I haven't seen a sniffer dog in a long time. Thankfully they don't pick up on my small stash and I get out of there as quickly as I can. The moist, warm air hits me.

If you want to pay only $10 for the shuttle to Antigua, you have to wait for at least three passengers to join the service. One guy is already waiting. I join him. More flights land, people come out of arrivals, but no one is going to Antigua by shuttle. After at least thirty minutes waiting, we decide to jump on a taxi that has agreed to take us for $20. We sit in the back of the taxi. There's a Covid divider between us and the driver. Faisal, that's the name of my fellow traveller, is a young vlogger from Algeria who has travelled extensively and is planning to travel most of Central America on this trip. In the back of the taxi, he starts to record a short video so suddenly I have to say hi to his followers! What a strange way to start this trip!

A first glimpse of Guatemala passes us by in the hour-long drive to Antigua. Spaghetti junctions of electricity cables slice the deep blue sky in the midday sun. I smile inwardly as I absolutely love the jumble of cables! I don't know why. We get to Antigua, the city where cars drive super slow on the cobbled streets, there are no traffic lights(!) and beggars stand on street corners waving a white flag.

We take Faisal to his hotel, then I finally reach my destination, Casa Gitana, where I am greeted by Carlos. I am the only guest, and the first since Covid started, so Carlos upgrades me to a room rather than the dorm I had booked. The room is super nice and comfy. I love the colours and the tiled floor. I am super happy here. There is one long-term guest at Casa Gitana, Anacleto, an old Italian guy (I know, what are the chances). Anacleto is clearly ill, liver problems. But he is stuck here. He's been here for 40 years and doesn't have enough funds to go back to Italy, it seems. It's rather sad. It also brings to my mind a comparison with the life I left behind, living and sharing with Hugh. It's funny that I've come all this way only to end up sharing the accommodation with an older man. You couldn't make things like these up!

29/01/ 21

Yesterday afternoon I went up the Mirador, a steep hill on the side of the town. It is a viewpoint with a huge cross at the top. Steps snake around the steep hill and, with a mask on your face, it is heavy going. But it's lovely and cool, as you are sheltered by the tall trees forming the wood. It is a refreshing respite, although you are going at full power to be able to negotiate the hill. Anacleto said it would be dangerous up there, but so far nothing has been. Everyone is nice and I have not felt threatened.

From the top of the hill, the town spreads below you, with its cobblestoned grid system and square buildings with generous internal courtyards. The whole town is nestled between three active volcanoes, two of which are visible from here and seem to cradle Antigua in a smoky embrace. Pacaya volcano, on the right, is puffing plumes of smoke. I take it all in as two hippies are busking. She looks like Yoko Ono: Japanese, large hat, playing the egg, whilst the guy is playing guitar and singing a sweet revolutionary blues in Spanish which is really soothing. I realise this is the first time in a year that I'm getting to enjoy any live music, due to Covid. I spark up a joint while a Mexican looking dog with its wrinkly frown is sleeping at my feet, in the shade of the wall where I am sitting. I study the town below, lost in thought and time and also consider what a productive morning it's been: I was looking for Willie the barber, but I found Willie the dealer instead, on Fourth Calle, so I scored some neat happy grass. Later I also found Willie the barber and finally got rid of my lockdown surplus hair. The barber shop had wooden panels, big 50's chairs, Spanish music blaring through the speakers and I got a very nice haircut from a young guy whilst we chatted in Spanish. I totally enjoyed that!

Here in Antigua everyone wears masks, including quite small children, but everything is open. Last night, as I was having dinner at Frida, a Mexican restaurant where they actually had club music and a proper party going on upstairs, I realised it had been a year since I last had eaten out! ... Really, apart from the masks and hand sanitiser everywhere, Antigua is leading a normal life, minus the tourists. There are very few of us here.

As I was strolling back to my accommodation, under the porticoes in the Parque Square, charity food was given out to the poor (who had suddenly appeared). The volunteers also sang uplifting songs to them accompanied by a guitar. At the end everyone clapped. Then, two police pickup trucks with flashing green and red lights showed up and summoned everyone home as it was 9 pm, curfew in the times of Corona is 9:30 pm.

I went back to the hostel and there was a huge full moon. In the pitch-black, starry sky, it stood right above my head, framed by the banana tree on one side and the roof of the building on the other.

This morning it was still sitting there, just a little further left, but this time the sky was light blue at dawn.

30/01/ 21

Carlos has helped me to organise an excursion to the volcano Pacaya. We were trying to organise it for tomorrow but then he came up to me and told me that there was a space today at 3 pm. So, I said I'd go. They came to pick me up with a shuttle, then we went to pick up a couple of French girls on the outskirts of town, then back into town to pick up a Swiss couple. After that, we drove out into modern Guatemala, the steep tarmac snaking through the hills, heavy with pick-up truck traffic loaded with people in the back. Yellow road signs, red curbs and Taco Bells, this is America.

As we approach the volcano, the guides tell us that to see the lava up-close we need to take a different route, costing 50 quetzals extra each, we begrudgingly accept. Once at the base of the volcano, we meet Connie, our Guatemalan tiny lady guide with silver stars encasing her teeth. We start some serious climbing on the pumice rock. "Mountain goat-ing", as I like to call it. It's hard going but exhilarating.

The volcano is full of people, it's like a party in Ibiza with people checking out the sunset and the clouds below, the ghostly, majestic mountain range populating the background from afar. To the right, at closer distance, volcano El Fuego is splashing lava and right above us a new crater on Pacaya is spitting out hot bubbles as incandescent rivers come down the side of it, almost on us. We watch, spellbound, amongst smells of food being cooked and shoes melting on the hot stones. It is busy and, as we wait to negotiate some narrow paths on the slippery rocks, we have to watch out where we stand, as some spots are really too hot to stand on. At the beginning of the absent, as we were going up the volcano, a chilly wind had started to gather strength and we scrambled to put all our layers on, but as soon as we got closer to the crater, man it was hot!

Before coming back down, we had marshmallows cooked on the mountain side, as the sun got replaced by a thousand stars first, followed by a big fat orange full moon. I had carried all the sound recording equipment with me, expecting total silence and a chance to record a volcano eruption. Not the case. This place is very much loved by Guatemalan and tourists alike, it reminded me of watching the sunset at the temple of Hampi in India.

31/01/21

I didn't mind keeping Anacleto company (although he is a bit depressing) and starting this trip in a somewhat quiet way, but four days here is enough and now I'm ready to move on. Where am I going? Lake or beach? the transport availability has chosen for me. Secretly, I guess I wanted to "beach" it, but it's looking like I'm going to the lake after all.

I haven't booked a room. I'm assuming it will be very easy to find something. I hope I'm right. Day four, I am already breaking my own rules number one and two: Don't arrive anywhere in the evening (I should get there at 5:30, technically there is still light) and always have accommodation booked for the first night so you have a destination when you arrive somewhere new.

To kill some time before travelling to Lake Atitlan I visit the modern art museum. I really enjoyed the painting made with chalk over a waxy canvas. Then I have an orange juice and a croissant in a café' at El Parque, comfortably sitting on a cushioned sofa, fans whirling under a canopy of painted trees on the ceiling. I watch the world go by; time is tolled by the churning noise of the circling fans.

02/02/21

I arrived at San Pedro, lake Atitlan, at 6:30 p.m. I'm staying at a place called Casablanca. They gave me a great room, two windows facing the lake. It's beautiful, the light constantly changing over the water and mountains all around. Twelve towns are distributed around the lake so at night there are pretty lights in the distance. Casablanca has hammocks, a restaurant under a canopy, a pool table and many chill-out areas. It's very nice.

I had a bitty night because I had had a few beers. Earlier in the evening I had bumped into the Swiss couple from the Volcano trip, and we had dinner and a pleasant evening together. I was also woken up by loud Spanish music blaring out of the mountains all around till 2:00 a.m. I hope it was a one-off party and not something that happens every night.

This morning I woke up early, had breakfast, took my dirties to the laundry and headed off to check out the beach at the left of my hostel: washer women are hard at work knee-high in water beating the clothes on smooth rocks purposely placed. Fishermen are tending to their boats. I walk to the far end. A dog comes to hang out with me for a while, while I bask in the morning sun. Then I go for a walk around town and book some Spanish classes. San Pedro is a tiny town, one narrow lane follows the contour of the lake, shabby buildings protrude over it, wood, cement, paint (there are loads of paint shops as here they hand-paint their shop fronts and signage) small gardens with banana trees and hammocks, bars and eateries dot the place.

At 2:00 p.m. I go for my first class with Lorenzo. Three hours of conversation and grammar. I have been wanting to do this for many years. The class is outside by the lake in the sunshine: I am very happy I'll be doing this all week.

After class, I go for a beer at the tiny bar on the right just after the hill and I order a Gallo, it's a foreigners' bar, I'm bound to score. I sit outside, close to two guys with an acoustic guitar and a dog. I offer them a tuner, which is an app on my phone, whilst their dog barks madly. Then I ask for some pot and (another!) William comes along and says he can help with that. While he is gone, I chat to the two buskers from Nicaragua, Stephen and Frank about playing music with other people. I have a problem with that as I think I am not good enough to play with others but they're very encouraging! Sweet kids! When William comes back, I buy a humongous bag of grass. It's huge and it's not even that bad! I'm considering smoking it neat, like they do here. In Guatemala, and in America in general, people don't usually mix tobacco with their marijuana. There is a nice vibe at the bar, but tomorrow's class is at 8 a.m. so I'm going to bed early. So far, it's quiet around San Pedro. Who knows if it still has to kick off.

03/02/21

No, it didn't kick off! This place is really chill, I'm getting into it. I wake up just before seven, a soft light kissing the mountains, the lake is still, glasslike. Last night I bought some cornflakes and almond milk so I venture into the back of the hostel looking for a spoon and a bowl since no staff are around to help this early. I find the items in the dingy kitchen. In the sink, I wash the bowl of all the black dust and have a lovely breakfast. It's the first time in three weeks I have almond milk and flakes. The almond milk is UHT, but I'm pleasantly surprised by the taste.

It's nice and cold as it has been chilling all night in the hostel's fridge, delicious!

It's cold in the early morning and I'm wearing all my layers. I go to class on the lake, it's so peaceful and beautiful. I learn loads, make loads of conversation and halfway through class we get offered coffee and a lovely fruit salad with papaya, melon and banana. I'm really enjoying these classes, but I've been given lots of homework for tomorrow.

I go back at 11 to try and join Cristina's Pilates class on zoom live from Rome, but the Wi-Fi is too slow. So, I change into my swimwear and walk to the end of the town to the tiny beach I found yesterday and go for a swim in the lake. I think it's the first time I swim in a lake. Or if I have done before, I don't remember. Some kids are swimming. I dip my toes in the clear water. It's quite cold but not too bad. Eventually I dive in and have a very short swim. There are some green algae in this lake, and I don't fancy crossing them (I read about these algae on my travel guide). Tomorrow I'll pick up a different spot, so I can swim further and longer... Anyway, it is so nice and really hot, so I end up having two more swims. There are loads of birds around this lake. Circling over the volcano, what looks like eagles to me (they're actually condors, I think). On the lake, elegant white birds with long necks stand on the water. Cute little ones scour the beach and butterflies all shape and sizes flutter about chasing one other. I want to swim every day if I can. The lake is hot and calm during the day, but early afternoon, with no fail, the wind rises over the lake cooling the whole thing and creating waves on the water. So, the best time to go swimming I figure is 12-ish, like today.

As I was sunbathing, a lady who had been washing clothes not too far away from me, passed me by and told me she liked my natural hair. My hair is pretty grey. Her Hair was not. She said her son wants her to dye her hair and she doesn't want to. She showed me her greys, just three or four strands. Difficult to say how old she was, as she was missing quite a few teeth. But anyway, she almost had no greys.

In the evening I scored more pot and had a beer with a crazy guy, Juan, another pot dealer I met.

04/02/21

I wake up early, it is warmer than yesterday. My almond milk is held hostage in the locked fridge, so I am unable to have breakfast. There is no one around apart from a guest I've never seen before who is taking pictures. I wash my face and brush my teeth, then I spark up on the hammock outside my room to kill the extra time before class. As I am there taking in more and more details of life on the lake, I see a bird, the head impossibly small, and I can't contain my excitement. I look closely through the foliage, yes, it is a hummingbird! So delicate and fast. A precious moment. Stupidly, I decide to go for my phone to take a picture and by the time I get it out, the bird is gone, and I have missed valuable seconds in the company of this cute little bird. Hopefully there will be more.

In the afternoon I take the lancha (a boat) to San Marco. Riding in the boat on the lake is very special and San Marco is very beautiful, totally surrounded by lush flora. It's quiet, peaceful, perfect and a magical town with special energies but it feels very touristic as it's full of foreigners with their yoga mats and hippies hanging about. I have a spliff and take a stroll on the tiny beaches by the side of the town. Then I chat to Juan, an American fireman from Nevada, and later, as I wait to board the boat back, I have a long chat with the boat captain. He tells me about the nice black beach of San Pedro, La Fincha and we exchange numbers so perhaps we can go there together sometime. We chat on the pier for a long time until three more people and a dog heading to San Pedro finally turn up, rescuing me from the wooden pier.

I think as a solo traveller and a tiny woman, I'm getting the best prices. I often see people being charged more than me (everyone gets charged differently here).

On my way back home, I bump into William who's snorting coke on the side of the road at 4 pm. This place is getting crazier by the day.

05.02.21

Today it is a beautiful day, they are cleaning the algae off the lake using a curious looking boat/rake thingy moved by propellers, like something you'd see on the Mississippi River. They scoop the algae out with a massive basket attached to the front of the boat. It's very entertaining to watch. Huge fountains of water shoot into the sky as the boat propels back and forth. The sea Gardener.

My swim is exhilarating. I am able to swim further out. Yes, it is cold, but pleasantly so. The water is not salty and it is much harder to swim, I think. Is it true? An old lady assured me the water was nice and I have to agree. I bumped into her on the beach. Skinny, topless and content, she was bathing and washing her clothes beating them on the stone as I swam. To my left, a guy was playing acoustic guitar on the rocks, inches away from the water.

I'm smoking a joint when he passes by to leave the beach, so he asks me for a joint which I give him, I have so much grass! Then he asks me if he can play me a song. He plays a song about San Pedro. I get most of the words and it's about being happy here, this song couldn't have summed up better the way I feel.

Anyway, his name is Louis, and we chat for half an hour or so, in Spanish. I think he understood most of what I said and I understood most of what he said. He spoke fast though, and I could not get everything.

Sitting by the lake, watching the world go by, just like in the song Louis sang, one of those majestic white cranes was standing on the water and I was pondering on how beautiful and mystic the whole scene was, condors overhead, when the white bird clumsily lost its footing and fell over into the water, how funny.

The sound design on the lake is pretty festive, with music, human activity, incessant rhythmic banging of the workers chiselling away at stone, but most of all, the birds chirping and whistling away, the weirdest whistles, of all lengths and pitches, long or syncopated and all these sounds come from everywhere, bounce off the mountains mixing each other with dogs barking and roosters crowing in the morning, with the sound of the tuk-tuks and moped traffic later in the day.

In the afternoon, craving a bit more nature, I venture to the outskirts of town where the chocolate and coffee plantations and the jungle begin. The road is very steep and quickly it gets very peaceful and indigenous. I meet an old campesino, smaller than me, dark skinned, thin, fedora hat and he's carrying on his back a huge piece of wood and coffee. We chat for a while; he tells me about the land and the past. I understand quite a bit and he's happy about that. He tells me that usually foreigners don't understand Spanish so he can never chat to them. He has cut the wood himself with a huge machete slinging at his side. He directs me towards La Fincha, apparently the best beach, but I stop a little short because it's too far, have a spliff surrounded by hummingbirds in a peaceful spot overlooking the lake, which here is much larger. Then I return into town. On the way I see many men pissing in the bushes, and I find that really funny, like it's a designated time or something. I unexpectedly stumble upon the main town square, garishly colourful with its gardens and the disproportionally humongous statue of San Pedro, complete with rooster by his side and huge keys to the city dangling at the other side. I decide to go for a pre-dinner beer. By this point I'm knackered so I head for the reggae bar. On the way, an Israeli man, flanked by menacing security guards, all dressed in black, face covered and heavily armed passes me by and it's a very strange sight in such peaceful settings and in such a narrow lane in a small town.

At the bar, four people from Guatemala City are going crazy, already very drunk, they start chatting to me. Vivi tells me she's a lesbian and likes red haired girls and because of this she would like to visit Scotland. She's young, a lovely smiley girl with a cute hat on. She's here with her mother, her mother's young boyfriend and another friend. They want me to go to Panacachel, on the other side of the lake, with them, but they're already so wasted, I don't think it's a great idea at all. Luckily, I have school in the morning, so I have a good excuse to decline the invitation although Vivi is very insistent. As they leave, Stephen and Frank and Jagger the dog turn up, and I go off with them to a bar named Sublime. Louis, who sang the song for me the other day is there too and also Sylvie, a girl from Sacramento. She looks dreamily into the distance of the lake as she's high on magic mushrooms. We all chat, they play guitar and sing. There are more people, a nice naked fire is bellowing on the terrace. We smoke and drink this very tasty drink called Quetzalteca which is rum based. It's really cheap and nice and everyone seems to drink it here. We end the evening on the pier. These boys from Nicaragua are very cool. They are taking the time to teach me Spanish and come and find me every night as they know I am alone. They told me so, as they said they couldn't find me the night before.

I realised today I could stay here a lot longer as I have hardly discovered San Pedro and I haven't visited the other towns around the lake at all, but the ocean also is calling... I haven't made up my mind, but I think I will go. I'm thinking I can return here if I have time, and maybe rent a house. That would be cool. I'm considering renting pretty much straight away at El Paredon, my next destination, if I like it and decide to stay there.

06/02/21

Waking up on the lake is always special and different. This morning a hummingbird kept coming back at the tree right outside my window and treated me to a big show. I even had time to take a few snaps, it was there for such a long time.

During the day, I have a couple of really good swims at the lake. Two American girls arrive at the hostel, one of them is called Marina! What are the chances.

I have a great burrito at the vegetarian café two stories up overlooking the lake, then head into town for the night. It's the weekend and the town suddenly swells up with locals. I end up at the 420 bar where a DJ is playing some good tunes and dance 'till they close. I meet Paula from Spain, Rosita and baby Lucy. Rosita is beautiful, she looks like a Madonna, in a woolly shroud, cradling the baby. She runs the famous pizzeria in San Pedro (I haven't been there yet myself) With her DJ/chef husband Manny.

Stephen, Frank and Jagger the dog turn up and, at the end of the music, we decide to go back to someone's house to smoke, drink, listen to music and do some edibles. I meet Hannah from Cardiff, she speaks Spanish very well and we talk about how she's embarrassed by the fact that most Brits are so lazy about learning languages. She freaks out because I speak a few Welsh words. She is travelling with an American girl called Montana and, since the fact that they are called Hannah Montana is clearly very amusing, they have decided to travel together. This is my first proper night out in Guatemala, pretty cool.

07/02/21

I woke up with a hangover, so I take it slow today. The philosophy here seems to be "have fun and be happy". Because you never know when it's going to end. Living so close to all of these volcanoes gives you such an outlook, I guess. People also seem to be very religious: most of San Pedro's buildings are painted with religious slogans. They are almost everywhere.

Life by this lake is so, so mellow. After some serious mountain goat-ing I reach a secluded spot on the rocks. I'm so hung over and don't think straight and in leaving the hostel, I decided I would not go for a swim today so I didn't pack my bathing suit in my bag, but I packed my harmonica instead. I am sitting on the rocks, this is a marvellous day, dipping my feet in the water and I try the harmonica a little bit. I must be extremely relaxed here if I manage to play with people relatively close! Anyway, at some point it gets so hot I just have to strip naked and go for a swim in my pants. That's unheard of, if you know me, an incredible achievement. Normally, I always wear shorts on the beach and here I am, alone on the rocks in my pants, having a swim with my boobs out. Astonishing! The water is the best it's been all week. Maybe I shall stay here for longer but this morning I've booked my ticket to El Paredon. I can always come back. Most likely I will. I can totally see myself renting a small house on the lake for at least two weeks, going swimming every day. The quiet houses are close to la Fincha. And it seems that most people who actually rent homes do so in that area.

I'm falling in love with my life at the moment. I have been away for three weeks now, just over 10 days of proper travelling (if you don't count being stuck in Naples) And I already feel free and can totally see myself continuing like this for a long time, something has melted away. Like it always does, after a few weeks on the road. And reality takes a new, slightly liquid form full of possibilities.

10.02.21

I arrived at El Paradorn two days ago. On Monday I woke up leisurely, had breakfast and hung out on the lake till departure time. The lake was just awesome, amazing temperature and really tempting but I had no time for a swim, so I just dipped my feet in the water during my stroll. Then I got to the pier and caught the boat to Panacachel. The lake was motionless and beautiful. The boat stopped at four pueblos to pick up passengers and I got to see more of this stunning lake. At one of the stops a puppy jumped on and we had to alert the captain as he was leaving with the puppy on board. Poor Perrito, probably waiting for his owner. On the boat there were a few French backpackers and a few local women with their super-bright bags of intricate design, wide belts holding long, colourful skirts, impractical for stepping into the boat and over its seats.

I have to kill an hour at Pana, so I skin up on the pier. Here I have the opposite view of the lake, pointy volcano perfectly framed at the centre of the view, the muelle in the foreground, picture perfect. I have a smoothie in the shabby looking comedor and strike a conversation with the chef and her daughter. She is 10, the daughter, playing with her little sister Irene. In a few minutes Blanca arranges Irene's hair in an intricate plait. Blanca has a very long ponytail. She tells me she would like to visit Paris and the Eiffel tower.

Finally, the shuttle arrives and there's only another passenger. She is a very fit lady, smiley, curly hair, dark skinned and piercing green eyes. We leave Pana and the lake behind, a little sad and also excited. We rise up through mountain roads, the clouds are below us, it's difficult at times to tell if you're looking at the sky, clouds or water. From up here the size of the

lake becomes clear. We are so high up, the road hugging the mountain, my dad would love this drive. In the four-hour journey I learn that the other passenger is called Stephanie, she is Guatemalan/German and has lived in Panacachel for the last 20 years. She runs a paragliding business with pilot/partner Christian and they have an 11-year-old son Liam. It's the first time she leaves the family behind for some well-deserved and needed R&R, and she is understandably torn by different feelings. We hit it off straight away because she's incredibly friendly and nice, so I have hit jackpot because now I'm hanging out with a local who knows El Paradorn well as she's been there many times.

As we leave the high altitude behind, a sticky humid heat hits. We are at ocean level. Stephanie is staying at a very chill place, so we decide that I'm going to stay there too. Surf camp is the first place to have been built on the beach and owner Rafa, who I am yet to meet, built it all on his own. It's not on any website because he wants to keep it authentic and won't just have anybody booking. I've decided I'll stay here paying five days at the time.

This town is tiny, one main tarmac-ed road and three more parallel sand paths, crossed maybe 20 times by sand and dust tracks creating blocks with simple houses made of breeze blocks, with patios in front and roofs made from dried palm leaves and wood. They're very beautiful, tall, pointy structures. Hammocks swing everywhere on patios and inside houses. Many buildings have murals on them. In San Pedro the murals depicted indigenous scenes or had religious content, here they are more nature oriented, with pictures of hummingbirds and other birds, flowers and ocean scenes.

Rafa's place is beautiful and peaceful. Everything is handmade using natural materials: wooden huts, sculptures, door handles, toilet paper holders made with driftwood, outside showers. There are hammocks, plants to give shade and a large wooden platform facing the ocean where one can do yoga, and lots of yoga mats.

Stephanie shows me the town, we enquire about some room for me to stay a bit more long-term and Angelica, the owner of the corner shop, introduces me to a couple of locals who show me some very basic rooms. Just a mattress in a windowless room and space outside with a hammock and outside toilet. Dirt cheap but really a bit depressing. Maybe I still have to get used to the look of things but no, I don't want to take this room. I rather pay a bit more and stay at Rafa's if I can. Stephanie also introduces me to other friends: Carla and daughter Sophie, who just moved here from Antigua and Matt, a British man who is here with his teenage daughters and are renting a beautiful house on the beach for a week. He's been living here for 20 years and is building some sort of alternative community in the jungle and growing cocoa close to Semuk Champey, a location I plan to visit. I might volunteer in his Cocoa farm. I need to enquire more about it…

At sunset the sun dips down perfectly and at night I fall asleep to the waves. Next morning, I go for a long walk on the beach. This beach is straight and immense, it goes on forever, I've never been on a beach that vanishes into the horizon. The ocean is calm and the Pelicans skim the water in a long line of up to 15 birds all perfectly following each other, flying right on the crest of the waves, expert flyers, agile on the water. A beautiful spectacle, the beach almost deserted, little birds on stick-thin legs patrol the water edge looking for food, running back-and-forth with the waves, and crabs dart about diagonally, all very amusing, the light is silvery pink.

After breakfast we go for a swim, the ocean is not too rough so we are able to break through the waves to get to where the water is still, and it's almost magical. Surfers dot the place, a strange calm and silence, after battling the pounding waves to get there. You still have to be careful though, as, all of a sudden, a big set of waves is still going to creep up on you with a certain regularity. Stephanie has to shout at me to watch out twice as I'm not used to it and when the sea gets calm, I start swimming normally like I would do in the Mediterranean. No, here you always have to keep an eye on the waves, always! The ocean is powerful and tiring so after a lovely long swim, we return to the beach. Later on, we sip wine on the hammocks, chatting and smoking all afternoon. At sunset we take a walk looking for the mouth of the canal, which runs right beside the beach. It reminds me of Agonda beach in Goa, with the mangrove. It's very beautiful. We are treated to another perfectly round orange ball quickly disappearing at the edge of the sea.

Pretty, colourful butterflies at Surf camp flutter about the place at eye level, sometimes seeming to accompany me for a bit of the way as I walk through the garden to go to the toilet. Guatemala is a country of one ply toilet paper. You know you are in a poor country when you only find this type of toilet paper. Which is perfectly adequate, may I add.

11.02.21

It's a bit cloudy this morning, I decide to go for a walk on the other side of the beach. I have the whole place to myself. The ocean is very calm this week, very tempting to try some surfing, but I'm not quite ready yet. It's good for swimming too though.

I have breakfast with Stephanie and Lola the chef organises a tuk-tuk for us to go 15km to the nearest cashpoint. The single road is straight, ocean on one side, canal on the other, cows graze in the fields and shade under the palm trees herded by rancheros with Stetson hats riding horses. On our way back, we check a house out. I might move there next week. The room is really nice, spacious with two windows, outside toilet and a hammock in the patio, next to a big family. It might be a great way to spend a week (or two if I like it) in full immersion once Stephanie goes (I would certainly learn a lot of Spanish here with this family)...

I will be able to stay here at El Paredon as long as I have pot. It's true that there's almost nothing here, it's even hard to get Rizlas or tobacco. And I am yet to meet a dealer! When I was leaving San Pedro, waiting on the muelle, I met Jose, one of the dealers and he told me I would not find pot here and he was insisting I should buy more from him. I didn't believe him of course, in my experience up until now it has been dead easy to score, and I thought he was just saying that to get more business. I already had quite a lot of grass on me and didn't fancy travelling with more on (we didn't get stopped on the journey down here, but I got apprehensive every time I saw police). So, I said no but now I'm starting to believe he was genuine and regret not buying some more from him. I might ask Matt to sell me some of his, if he's got any left, before he leaves tomorrow.

For the rest of the day, I have a couple of lovely swims by myself in the relatively calm sea, chat to a local family with 10 children, playing in the waves just like we used to as kids, running away from the chasing waves on the shore. I go back to camp to see my first two iguanas of the trip! Nice and big and lizardy! I do yoga for the first time on the platform, facing the ocean, feeling the breeze. This is awesome. relaxation time is amazing.

In the evening we go for a nice pizza at the Israeli place with Carla, her albino daughter Sophie, Matt and his two children as it's their last night. The low seating in this place is some sort of sofas made out of cement, really cool, kind of brutalist! The floor is just sand just like the roads outside. This town is built right on the beach. After, we go for a couple of shots of rum in a cool place with nice music and a young surf crowd, a nice evening. Stephanie and I go back home by the beach. Below the starry sky, silvery waves slide over the black sea, we find a slack line and we try it, I can only do 3-4 paces.

12/02/21

Because it's volcanic, the sand here is black, as black as Miseno's beach in Naples, which is also volcanic. This morning I went all the way where the sea and the canal meet. Here it's like another world. Many birds of all sizes including vultures and white cranes dot the place. At first, I thought they were a distant town. I followed the contour of the canal for a while where you can't hear the ocean any more but you get the sound of the river. The other canal bank is lined with mangrove and the canal splits up in many directions. There are mini-islands and sandbanks and many more birds, very pretty. I return home ready for breakfast. Stephanie explained to me an interesting fact about Lake Atitlan over breakfast. She said that the lake was very polluted before Corona. Since, it got cleaned up and new birds arrived including the elegant long necked white cranes! that's awesome.

I spend a pleasant evening going to a jam session, have a few drinks and meet a few people. The place is really nicely decked out, with tables, hammocks and a small stage with pretty lights, the crowd is nice, and we chat by the bar. I discover something that amuses me and intrigues me: apparently no Italian has settled here, and I could be the first! I'm not saying this is the place for me, it could definitely be if I were to take up surfing. But the thought of having found somewhere so nice, with no Italian settlers yet, where I could be the first, has a strange charm about it.

13.02.21

Ha ha! this morning, after breakfast where I chatted with the new guests, Alex and Kate from Chile and the States, Marina, the American girl who I met in San Pedro showed up at Surf Camp with her friend! Small world.

After a few swims, (the ocean is calm again today), I sit under the shady shack which is built in front of our camp. From where I stand, so far up on the beach, it looks like you can see the curvature of the Earth, but not like you "see" it in Ravello, looking over the "window over infinity" of Villa Cimbrone, where it seems to round at the edges. Here it runs in front of you, almost flat. (I chuckle as I consider that maybe those people who think that Earth is flat, have been looking at this kind of horizon).

I decide to stay here at Surf Camp 4 more days. The location and facilities have won over the full immersion stay with the local family. I have decided I can do Spanish in other ways; I just have to apply myself a bit more.

14.02.21

I wake up early, my calves too painful from yesterday's walk. I walked a lot on the beach yesterday, maybe three hours altogether. I opt out my usual morning walk and instead do some early morning yoga facing the ocean, which is lovely. Again, it's pretty calm today. I go for a swim before breakfast, a few surfers are out. I break through all the breakers, then the sea is calm. I can't feel sand under my feet. It's the first time since I arrived that I have a swim in open sea. I'm learning to swim in the ocean, respect it and keep the uneasiness at bay. Meanwhile Europe is gripped by winter. It's snowing even in Carovigno, Apulia. Hugh sent me a picture, very pretty, but poor Hugh, it must be very cold...

Marina invites me to do some yoga on the platform before lunch and it's nice to practice with other people, after such a long time! In the afternoon, five of us go paddle boarding in the mangrove with Sean and his handsome dog Ziggy. We let the river's current take us until we turn into one of the canals. The narrow canals open through the thick mangrove, and it's pretty magical: birds, crabs and other animals live here and if you are in front of the convoy you get a chance to see more wildlife. When I was in front, I saw flying fish! As we paddle through, sometimes the fin of the board gets stuck in the mangrove roots and branches below the water and Sean has to come to free us. Clearings in the mangroves are picture perfect opportunities. As we reach the open river once more, we let the current take us as we take in our surroundings, peacefully lying on our backs on the boards, whilst lanchas pass us by slowly.

At sunset, Carla, Sophie and I take a long walk to the boca-barra, where the river meets the sea as there is a bonfire for Max's birthday, he's the owner of a bar called Kawama. Twenty surfers drink and chat and dance around the fire. Momo, the Canadian bartender of Kawama, comes to chat to us. We don't stay long, but enough not to be eaten alive by all the mosquitoes as it happens any other night. We walk back in the pitch dark, the silvery waves and the amazing starry night as a backdrop. In the dark, we play I spy with my little eye in

Spanish. It's one of Sophie's favourite games but since we're in the dark everything we spy is black.

15/02/21

Most people have gone, it's Monday. The beach is empty at sunrise. It's beautiful and pink and orange, and also, it's the first time I managed to catch it. Carla and I go for a walk before breakfast to the barra and decide it's actually a very good swimming spot for young Sophie so when we return, we pick her and the two tiny Chihuahua dogs they have, Papa and Tango, up and go back there by boat. After haggling with the boatman, we finally board. The river trip is lovely. On the narrowboat covered by an awning, we strike conversation with Jorge the driver. He tells us about a turtle tour, so we decide to go tomorrow. I am so happy about it! a dream come true. Finally! I was changing my mind about going to Monterico to the turtle sanctuary and was getting a bit depressed thinking that the turtles keep eluding me! But no more! Tomorrow is my day! I'm quite confident we'll see one. Last night, as we were going to the bonfire, we saw a big dead turtle shell and skull washed up on the beach.   We swim in the river for a while and play with Sophie. I can finally have a good, proper swim in calm waters. we decide to come here every morning with Sophie, early, when it's not too hot, so we can walk here. Carla and I have hit it off, I try to speak Spanish as much as possible… Perhaps I'll stay here a bit longer, now we found a good swimming spot.

When we return, I sit on the beach looking at the ocean for a while. I'm the only person on this kilometres-long beach. This is a pretty special moment to savour and take in. A cool breeze makes sitting here very pleasurable. I have watched the waves so much this week, that when I close my eyes at night, I still see them crushing on an imaginary beach, the fantasy made more vivid by the sound of the real waves actually there, only a few meters away. It feels like when you drive for far too long on the motorway and when you stop, tired and go to bed, shut your eyes and you still see a straight road and cars driving on the back of your eyelids.

Speaking to Carla and her daughter is great. I think I will stay here a bit longer because it's like having one-to-one lessons talking to a like-minded, sweet person. Today I discovered she smokes! So, we can definitely hang out a little more! And I think it will help her as well, with childcare or sharing some expenses...

From my hammock at night, I can really appreciate the garden, the array of plants and lush foliage, the borders and paths made out of recycled materials such as bottles, the different shades, hidden corners. I particularly enjoy walking barefoot on the soft sand or grassy path knowing that I'm not going to hurt my feet, peering through different leaves at a beautiful black, twinkling sky. I think I can make out the Milky Way.

I'm getting used to the rhythm of this place, when to look for shade or when it's time to escape from mosquitoes to the windy beach, and I am slowly falling into complete comfort. (I even played some harmonica in the hammock today). My bed is like a sanctuary, with it's very efficient mosquito net. I go to bed every night knowing that this place is bug free and I sleep extremely well, cradled by the sound of the waves and woken up early each morning by the roosters.

15/02/21

This morning I'm so excited, Carla, Sophie and I are going to see the turtles! It's something I've always wanted to do, see them in the wild. Since, as a child, I saw a black-and-white picture of my grandad, who was a big man, riding one, I think in Africa. Of course, it's appalling that he was doing such a thing, but they were very different times then.

We take the narrowboat with Jorge. I bought cookies to share with everyone. (I discovered the panificadora of the town, the bakery. They make lovely cookies and simple cakes just like I like them, no cream or anything too fancy. There is only one type of bread sold here, a soft, sweet long hotdog type of bun. Better stick to tortillas! Although sometimes, to save up, I'll make my own avocado and tomato sandwich…

The trip on the river is always great, full of birds. The pelicans resting on the sand are now more recognisable than when in flight (I have a Disney idea of pelicans, but their beak is almost never enlarged, it swells up only when they have fish in it. Otherwise, it looks like a pretty slender beak).

 When we get to the Bocabarra, where the river meets the ocean, we don't go to the ocean as I expected but we continue on the canal until Jorge switches off the engine and sure enough after a while the turtles start popping out for air making loud puffing noises as they breathe with their Mr Magoo faces. They are pretty big and it's quite magical although the water here is rather murky due to the black sand so you can only see them when they come up for air. I am shocked as I didn't know they would be found here but Jorge explains that they come to the canal because the water is calmer than the open sea. There are many turtles (unless it's always the same ones we keep spotting) I dive in the cool canal to try and swim a bit closer to them and one of them comes quite close!

It's lovely swimming in the river being transported downstream by the strong current knowing that at any moment a turtle head could pop up very close. On the way back, we stop at a lovely beach on the river so Sophie can swim a bit. There are lots of birds, sand dunes, and they collect salt here on some flat sandbanks behind us. We managed to see a lot more of the mangrove on this trip, it's really beautiful. this morning gets a 10 out of 10.

Now I'm sitting at the desk of my cabana, the church on the other side of the street has started a service. They have a very unlikely live band. A seven-year-old kid on drums, a very old man on bass and an old lady singing so desperately out of tune, I think she's taking the Mickey. It's very entertaining as it only lasts one hour. As it's so bad, I decide I can start playing the harmonica alongside it from my hut, it's fun!

VIEW FROM WINDOW – SURF CAMP

I like that in Guatemala the food is served slowly. When I go to dinner at the comedores I usually bring a book and, if I time it right, I don't get eaten by mosquitoes while I wait for my food and I feel quite a pleasure in fact, in the waiting, knowing that it's been lovingly prepared from scratch.

Tonight I'm dining at Sandra's. There is a group of about 10 surfer-girls being very merry. At some point they connect the speakers, and a proper party begins, they sing along and dance around, even on tables and chairs at some point! A big group of Guatemalan joins in and it's very amusing to watch. Then Donna, a British surfer I had previously met with Stephanie, comes up to say hello and find out a bit about me. She is very nice and invites me over to the party, but I decline as they are all very drunk and I'm not, swell party though, it puts a smile on my face.

Fun fact, all the Brits I meet tell me that I have a British accent like they almost can't tell I'm Italian, this is odd because you can totally hear I'm not British.

18/02/21

They have cancelled my return ticket!! Next available flight is in July. I let the news sink in, the more it does, the happier I am! I can take it real slow now.

El Paredon is a town in the making. It is pretty exciting to witness such a small place taking shape. Sad too, as I know in a few years this will be like Tulum in Mexico has become. I am blessed to have been here at this time. I guess there aren't many places like this around. The main difference between here and say, a small town like Carovigno in Italy, is that here the population is young, amongst the local there are many children and the tourist/foreigner population that is making a life here is predominantly made up of young surfers, not old expats.

Stephanie left this morning so today I get Surf Camp all to myself to enjoy! (Before new guests arrive), indeed it feels like I have the whole El Paredon to myself, the beach is also deserted. I go for a couple of nice swims (the waves are not too wild) and I step on something alive as big as my foot (Which is not a big foot, I know) Man, this ocean is full of big creatures! Later I decide to practice some harmonica under the canopy just in front of Surf Camp. I feel relaxed playing here because, aside the fact that there is no one, the ocean roars cover the sound of my playing (or so I like to think). The sea is so relatively flat and inviting, blue, glistening in the sun, and there is no one in sight on the beach, I'm playing the harmonica looking at the sea, when suddenly, I notice something in the water. It's not a surfer (it would be very far) it's not a person (thank God, as it would be way too far!) it's not a seabird. Hell, it's turtles! Bopping up and down in the distance. A spectacle just for me and the sound of my harmonica playing (which seems to be getting a bit better too!) ah! What a life!!

GARDEN AT SURF CAMP

19/02/21

More people arrived yesterday: Claudia, from Portugal. She has been hitch-hiking for the past year through central and south America. She came away from Europe just before Covid hit and doesn't plan to go back till the pandemic blows over. She is a nurse. Alberto, from Italy, and his girlfriend, they live in Antigua. We have dinner together at the camp, chat about travel, places, Covid and conspiracy theories. They are nice, interesting, well-travelled people but all this chat about serious stuff clashes with my mood and that of El Paredon. So, I have to tell them, "Please let's enjoy yourselves, that's why we came, enough talk about the real world." Or shall I say, the other world, as certainly this feels like real life now. For example, this morning I'm going to babysit Sophie. I'll be entrusted with her welfare after just a few days of knowing each other. So naturally and easily. This wouldn't happen in Europe, not this fast, certainly not in the UK.

I don't mind looking after Sophie as she is a sweet child, and today it is a bit overcast so I don't mind not going to the beach. These new arrivals, as lovely as they are, brought clouds and even four drops of rain! I know, because I was out recording sounds of the canal very early in the morning when it rained.

VIEW FROM 1ST CABAÑA – SURF CAMP

I babysat Sophie this morning for one hour, whilst Carla went to work. She had a client needing a haircut. It was fun hanging out with Sophie, we made drawings using the mobile phone. She is very good! In the afternoon I took Claudia to the BoccaBarra, to show her where the ocean meets the river. We chatted all the way, she's very nice. Obviously, she loved the place and we stopped at key points to soak in the scenery. The birds were a lot more active this evening, I told myself to come back at this time tomorrow to do some recordings. When we returned, Rafa the owner had arrived, and surf camp was full! I will have to play my harmonica on the beach!

VIEW FROM ROOM 2 – SURF CAMP

20/02/21

I moved room today. This is "unofficially" the last night here. Claudia wants to paint the town red, obviously. We go to Kawama for a few drinks, the music is good. We chat to a few people, including James from the States and Greg from "Chefs in flip-flops." But at some point, Max shuts the place down early because apparently the police are on the beach shutting parties down. After a while, we end up on the beach where we spot a group of about 20 Guatemalan and Hondurans. They have loads of booze, a massive 4x4 on the beach with a loud stereo and a very good vibe. Evidently the police didn't shut this party down! They're all very young (obviously) but the atmosphere is really cool. They offer us to drink beer and mescal and make a fire on the beach. Everyone is chatty, three queer guys from Antigua are very nice people and look after me all night; another guy called Daniel likes my haircut and he wonders if I dye my hair, I tell him "No, and you're not the first to ask", then he spends half an hour showing me pictures on his phone of when he dyed his hair platinum, bless him, so sweet. At 1:30 am I go home but Claudia stays behind.

21/02/21

Last day at El Paradorn. I wake up early and catch a lovely pink dawn. The beach is quite busy with people that never went to bed. When I return from my walk, I realise that last night, on leaving the beach, I picked up Claudia' sandals and not mine. Basically, I've lost my sandals! When I see Claudia staggering back in the morning, she tells me she's been looking for her sandals everywhere. I assure her I actually have them but that's no consolation for me, as this is now a confirmation that I have definitely lost mine as she hasn't got them. I settle for a quiet day arranging onward travel, when Carla and Sophie show up with a pair of new sandals for me! (They fit perfectly)! Que buena onda! Sophie made me a beautiful necklace with a fresh leaf, a 24-hour necklace. I went swimming with it on and it didn't break. We have a last dinner together and later we hang out on the beach looking for crabs by flashlight.

22.02.21

I can't believe I'm actually going today. The sea is just perfect (I know I say it every day, but today it is really nice). Everyone left yesterday, and you get that feeling that the place is all yours. I have a nice chat with dad on Whazzup as it's his birthday. Claudia and I decide to do some yoga together. She does a lovely gentle class which totally resonates with our surroundings and within me. Suddenly, as we are holding a triangle pose, a lovely hummingbird starts flying around the garden. It's a very special moment, especially because, as I am holding the pose, I don't get the urge to grab my phone to take a picture, but rather, I am extra present. Hence, I get to really savour the moment, the hummingbird is there for perhaps a minute.

I've had the best of times here. It's a really enchanted, calm place, with good people. I've made some good friends. I love Surf Camp's garden and I had this compelling urge to keep drawing it. (I haven't picked up a pencil since I was a teenager!)

I am off. Palm trees and cattle, dust roads, flat land and heat, then, all of a sudden, some mountains like crooked teeth sprout out of the ground, like towers made with wet sand. Now the trees are big and full of leaves, no more palm trees. The temperature drops and I am back in Antigua, at Carlo's place. I go out to shop around for shuttles to the jungle, and as I turn the corner, I bump into the Americans Marina and Liz eating an ice cream. Marina decides to walk with me and shows me around some places. (They have been living here for a month). It turns out they live literally one minute walk from me, on the same road! We visit a few travel agents and, in the process, since she is the millionth person to tell me I should go to the volcano Acatenango, well, it looks like I'm staying in Antigua for a few days and Wednesday night I will go to the volcano. I'm hoping to record a good soundscape but I'm dreading the cold.

24/02/21

So how was the volcano? You may ask, and the hike? The hike is tough. Very steep, at times it is hard to breathe due to the altitude. The path is slippery with rocks, and you better have a walking stick on this particular volcano, it really helps. The hike is beautiful, through thick rainforest, high up over the clouds. We make at least five stops plus one for lunch on our six hours climb to base camp. Twentytwo of us, mostly French, a couple of Germans and a couple of Americans. We all get on and help each other along the way. When we reach Base camp, the view is stunning. Left to right, Pakaya has river of red lava down its side (they closed it down now because it's too dangerous to visit up close, so I was lucky to go when I did). Then there is volcano Agua and to the right it is El Fuego, exploding with lava and big plumes of smoke every 20 minutes. What a show! The lava rises up to the sky then crashes down the side of the mountain in incandescent rivers. The ground shakes every time. It's cold up here at night. We have been given jackets, hats and gloves to keep warm. We have wine, hot chocolate and dinner by the fire and one of the French guys prepares a cheese fondue, 3000 Metres up! The local guides love it and play with the stringy cheese. It is fun to watch, they have never had it before, and they really like it. Well, it is very yummy. I have a tent on the edge of the mountain all to myself, and after a few minutes it's toasty and super comfy in my sleeping bag. I have a great night sleep. In the morning the cloud is too thick, so most of us decide to miss out on another hour and a half of hiking to reach the very summit of Acatenango for sunrise. My bed is too inviting.

We have breakfast by the fire, enveloped in thick cloud and mist. Everything is wet. Then we start descending the steep, slippery mountainside. Going down the volcano is a completely different experience. This time enveloped in mist, only able to see the trees right around me, somehow my surroundings get more defined. I can appreciate the abundance of different plants, shapes, shades of green, silver and white, mosses attached to lianas, lichen attached to ancient trees. Decay, dead trees, snapped, or shooting upwards, headless and dead, an eerie sight.

The hike down is slippery and at times the whole of our shoes would be submerged in dust and pebbles, sometimes we almost fall, or slide or fall right on our bum, unaided by the heavy load we are carrying on our backs. After a while, my legs feel like jelly and when we stop for breaks, they tremble. I never felt my legs like this before in my life. Mentally, going up was hard, coming down is unexpectedly even worse! At points I feel like I can't do it. One of our guides comes to chat to me so I don't think about it and sure enough suddenly I can see the entrance! It took 2 1/2 hours. I get home and I am dead.

Today I find it really hard to go down steps. I organise the trip for tomorrow as I'm going to the jungle. I meet with Parma, Karla's contact in Antigua. He's a nice guy, now I'm good to go, I haven't tasted the stuff, but I think it's okay. I smoked some of Karla's before and I am guessing and hoping it's the same.

The hiking group wants to meet up for drinks. I am half thinking of not going, when I bump into two of the French guys on their way there, so I go too. We end up in a very British bar, where they're even doing a pub quiz (ha!, so British!). We have a drink and a chat, which is nice, because we all got on really well over the last few days. Of course, they're a lot younger, but who cares, they are nice kids. In the pub, I also bump into Paris Milk, one of the gays who looked after me in El Paredon, and we spend five minutes chatting. I seem to keep bumping into people I have met before and they always seem happy to see me again and ask questions and really seem interested in what I am doing, in pure Latino fashion!

22/02/21

I travelled to Lanquin yesterday. We left Antigua, crawled up steep mountain roads, brown and dusty dark green, pines and another hundred species of trees, I wish I could name them. Nonetheless, a mountainous landscape. On the other side of the mountain, Ranchos, large hats, horses and cattle, then palm trees, jungle, humid heat, plants crawling onto other plants, all jostling for life. After eight hours, we take a last dirt road snaking down the mountain to Lanquin. Perched on the side of the mountain there are wooden shacks, Indios and tiendas, three or four steep roads fighting with the jungle around. People seem a bit different as I have a first stroll around town. They speak Mayan dialect more than Spanish here.

I am looking for tobacco. Rolling tobacco. There is none. I visit at least 15 tiendas. They look and study the packet of "señor Azteca" I am holding in my hand, but they shake their heads, don't have any. In the end I have to buy straight cigarettes. I find an old, small stone church, half dilapidated (but still functioning, I think). It dramatically stands thinly and precariously on the top of the mountain. Somehow, it speaks of suffering, it screams to the sky about the past. I don't know how or why I know this, nor do I know how to better explain it, but that's exactly how it feels, the church projects a kind of "still urgency" in the deafening silence of the sunset.

There is a market (dust and wooden shacks) and a square. To start, people don't seem to say hi when you meet them, as much as they do in other places. But I don't mind. As I walk and enter all the shops, they start warming to me. I find out where I'm going to have a haircut. They have some wicked haircuts here; I've asked around and I think I found who is the man behind them! My legs are still killing me from hiking Acatenango, so I'm going to take it easy for a couple of days here by the river. But I can't stay here too long, it's very expensive. And they play terrible music. I wish I could sit here listening to the jungle, but right now they are playing music. Luckily, I know they don't play it all the time.

RIVER AT EL REPOSO - LANQUIN

I went for a swim in the super cold river, how nice. The current is strong, but what is more striking, is that the water feels thick. I'm not jumping from the jetty, not today.

EL REPOSO - LANQUIN

01/03/21

Yesterday I went to Semuk Champey. What a place. The drive there, through thick jungle on dirt roads was great. Before getting my ride, I had to wait for one hour with Melissa, the fruit stall holder, also a big hustler! I met all her family. They also have a hotel which they hope to reopen next week.
The driver of the truck taking me there is 17 but he is very

capable! He leaves me by a hut close to the entrance of Semuk Champey and tells me he'll meet me here in three hours. I go in, steep steps made out of rocks lead to the mirador. What a view. Below, the river is gushing out of the mountains, then pools of limestone and waterfalls. A howler monkey perched on a tree starts its deafening call. Time stops and all of us below, share a moment. I go swimming in the pools, right in the gorge surrounded by beautiful trees and mountains. What a day! So much to take in, it's breath-taking.

At the end of the three hours, I go to the appointment spot and of course, the driver doesn't show up. It's very hot, so I ask the owner of the hut if I can wait under their shade. We have a chat, it is grandad Eric and grandma Estrella, 25-year-old Emily with a baby feeding at her breast, and Dylan, probably six or seven, doing some maths with grandad, lying down on a mountain of clothes on the floor, which I think they are trying to sell. Next door is Luz Maria, selling snacks. They are very sweet people; everyone is listening out for the cars coming up to the site. Time goes by and we are still conversing but inside I start panicking a bit (why did I pay in advance? So silly, I'm in the middle of the jungle! How long can I hang out with these nice people? I have no signal on my mobile, they have no phone! And so on) They tell me they know the guy who's meant to pick me up and they start asking other drivers if they have seen him driving here. Apparently, they have and, sure enough, eventually he comes, although very late. He says he had a puncture, which is highly possible on this road! On the way back through the jungle he blasts Spanish music out of the stereo. We chat about music. Suddenly an iguana chasing its meal is right in the middle of the road. Our arrival disturbs the pursuit, and the prey gets away. "We saved it!" Amrin shouts over the music. What a surreal moment.

This morning I went for a walk and the market was buzzing: food, bags, shoes, clothes, chocolate and beans on display on the floor and on wooden stalls. People everywhere, ladies in long skirts with colourful Guatemalan prints. I got some veg for

lunch, the barber was closed, and Melissa helped me to book a shuttle for tomorrow. She told me that yesterday there was a wedding, opposite her store, and everyone was stung by a swarm of bees. Including herself (When she first told me what happened, I misunderstood and thought she said she had been beaten up by one of the wedding guests, which was funny). She said the bees were a sign that the wedding was doomed.

Later at the hostel: I have a couple of lovely swims in the river and get talking to the other guests, three French people who met on this journey and are sharing a little bit of it together. I learn from one of them that the cocoa fruit, which is a big yellow pod, contains the seeds covered by a pulp which you can eat (it tastes of fruit, not chocolate). Then the seeds are dried and you can get cocoa, fascinating!... Suddenly a Finnish, a Guatemalan and a Spanish girl turn up and we have a bit of a fiesta. They have been travelling together for a while, hitchhiking. They are super chill and create exactly the vibe that this place was lacking. We smoke and drink till late by the river. The jungle is so humid, all my rizlas are completely wet and stuck together, as if a drink had been spilled over them.

Karry the Guatemalan, lost most of his clothes as they forgot his bag somewhere. I had been thinking of getting rid of some of my clothes and Karry is very tiny so when I hear this, I think this is the universe sending a sign, and I gift him a pair of shorts which fits him perfectly! He is very happy and so am I and my bag is slightly lighter! They fit him much better than they fit me. I have a private chuckle thinking I better not tell him that they are my mum's old shorts! As we chat, I discover he is from San Pedro, then I actually remember seeing him around there. He is quite easy to spot, notice and remember, with his long dreadlocks.

02/03/21

I was meant to leave today but the shuttle didn't go. Better really, I was too hung over and nauseous to take this ride through the jungle, I would've definitely felt sick on the way.

The stars at night are really close here in Lanquin.

EL REMATE

05/03/21

So, I have got the shits. I thought I was hungover from the drinks of the other night, but it's now clear it is something else as I've been ill for five days. Therefore, I haven't been writing, just trying to feel better. Travelling from Lanquin was not too bad, just a small sense of claustrophobia when we all got on the bus and started driving through the mountains. The landscape was slightly oppressive, and with the bus full, it took a while to get used to and the feeling only dissipated when we left the mountains behind. I knew at least ten people on the bus. I chatted to the two Canadians I met at the hotel the night before leaving and we shared a breakfast of Gallettas and Guatemalan chocolate. This was very coarse, shaped in a thin disc and had some other flavour in it, I think. I would like to try the plain one.

After ten hours of driving through a landscape of cattle ranches, horses and pasture with the odd palm thrown in, we get to El Remate. It's dark, so I don't appreciate it until next morning but they give me a lovely room instead of the dorm I had booked. As I open the door next morning, a hummingbird stares at me straight in the eyes and hovers around me for a while, the garden is lush, and we are a few steps from the lake. This place is awesome. We are right at the edge of the nature reserve, about half a mile from the small town. One road hugging the lake, and jungle on the other side. I go for a short early walk towards the reserve and as I approach it, a cacophony of sounds, howler monkeys in the distance and what seems to be hundreds of other animals, all calling. Amazing. Animals are not intimidated by man here. You do get a sense that you are in their space. This lake is warm, you get lovely sunsets, the town is nice, people are friendly. I will stay here a while.

I go to dinner at the small comedor at the other edge of town. I get served a lovely plate of food by a 10-year-old, Astrid, and chat to her 12-year-old brother for a while about school and life here. He goes to school once a week, fully masked, because of Covid.

At night I lie on the muelle looking at the stars, I can't really recognise the usual stars. The sky is full. On the motionless lake, the sky at night, or any other thing for the matter, is replicated perfectly, if somewhat "wavey" or "liquid". It looks lovely. This doesn't happen on the sea. Another difference, here there is no sound of waves. There are sounds of frogs and chirps and birdcalls, fireflies and crickets. I love walking at night along the single road. As the days go by, Mon Ami, where I stay, seems to get closer and closer to town whilst I wish for this walk to last a little bit longer each day.

07/03/21

Yesterday I met Emily, a true modern gadget girl from Guatemala City, complete with camera, tripod, phone and a smart watch. She was taking pictures on Mon Ami's colourful muelle. We spent all day chatting and swimming and we had lunch together. I like this passing by of people, dipping in and out of their lives, like a dip in the lake.

This morning I got up early and waited for Pulga to come and pick me up on his motorbike. He has a project, and I am going to check it out. We drive in the slightly chilly morning, nice to be on the scooter. We go to his house to pick up his kids, there are chickens and dogs. Pulga is a passionate conservationist. He has land with native plants, and he teaches kids about the environment, amongst other things. I spend the day with them playing and teaching an impromptu English class. Then they show me the rest of the jungle farm. Impressive, his cows, fed on sugarcane and other stuff, are the fattest I've seen during this whole trip!

I had come here with a view to moving to this farm in the jungle but it's really far from the lake! so I don't think I will. We decide to organise an English class on Tuesday with the kids; a bit mad really, as I'm not a teacher and I am not English, but why not, they have been hardly going to school because of Covid, they are lovely kids and I have time. Pulga is also a national park guide for El Mirador and works with documentary people sometimes so, who knows, maybe he can introduce me to someone.

08/03/21

I went to Tikal today (I feel a lot better!) With the collectivo, the public transport. I saw spider monkeys, howler monkeys, a huge snake (I'm sure it was dangerous) huge plants, millions of birds and of course the Mayan temples. A great day. I walked four hours in the jungle. I managed to record a Spider Monkey fight and a branch of a tree almost fell on me (I guess the monkey snapped it by jumping on it) In another instance, I am pretty sure that a spider monkey was chucking seeds at me (they were all getting dangerously close).   Alas, I didn't get a good sound of a howler monkey today, all day. At some point I recorded a family of at least six, jumping in the trees above for five minutes, but they didn't howl. When I returned home, I went to the cemetery at dusk, and yet they didn't come there either.

We have been getting ready for rain, people are dredging the canals dug in the ground outside the shops. I wonder how much rain is coming. Big canals for runaway water are visible everywhere here in Guatemala.

09/03/21

Last night I went to bed early. A few minutes after I did, I heard a great noise and thought half the roof of the cabaña had collapsed. Instead, it was "just" a tree crushing down and missing the house by millimetres.

It didn't rain; instead, I woke up to a beautiful day, a bit overcast but super warm. I swam all morning, beautiful, then went to teach English to Lander, the kid from the comedor. It went okay although he later said he has lots of homework at the moment, probably he doesn't want to do it again. Can't blame him, poor kid!

People in Guatemala are tiny, and some people look a lot younger than they actually are. An 18year old looks 10 and a seven-year-old looks 4. Is it malnutrition? There is also obesity. Many people are fat from a very sugary diet. The worst habits of the USA have trickled down it seems, but of course, also politics are to blame, as usual. Here in the Petén region, it's now a Covid red zone, but locals say that it's just a political game to get funds. I can believe it. I don't see families torn apart by death, and the cemetery doesn't have tombs from this year. Had Covid hit this community, the vibe would certainly be different.

DORM AT MON AMI'

10/03/21

I went to check out a couple of houses to rent, both really nice actually. One is a jungle hut right beside where I am staying now, and I love this area. The other is a second floor, view of the lake, good Internet and lots of hammock space in and out, but it's in town. I want to check out the one beside here again, it's a bit less comfortable but it has a lot of potential, I think. I also got offered a job in the pizzeria, taking orders. I might take it just to have something to do while I research filming opportunities.

Frogs ribbits at night, plus the tweets of other birds and chirps of crickets all going off at once sound like techno music. Add a faraway Spanish drumbeat and you have a tune. Funny how the cacophony of nature sounds always reminds me of techno music, with its sounds and rhythms, tones and timbres, its melodies and tunes.

11.03.21

Today I went to Flores, the Guatemalan version of the "old small town by the sea". Steps, narrow lanes and colourful houses strangled on a very tiny island surrounded by the lake Itzbal and connected to the mainland by a short bridge. It was extremely hot, and I saw fresh water turtles swimming in the lake and basking in the scorching sun all around it.   On the way back I rode on the bus with chickens. Then, as it was a perfect evening, I went swimming on the muelle with French botanist Jann and American Jinnie. They volunteer at the fincha Sol y Verde, a project beside Mon Ami. David the barman told us that a crocodile had been spotted around the corner at the biotope. Tomorrow I'm taking a walk there!... I think I'm going to rent the hut round the corner, this area is just too magical to go and stay in town.

12.03.21

It was lovely to walk with Jockey, the dog of Mon Ami, this morning. He's taken to accompany me for walks. I went for yoga on the pier of El Palomino which is abandoned and totally wild and gorgeous, full of birds and beautiful lily pads. The water was great. Later I went to teach English to two local girls, Michelle and Catalina, then I went to Sol y Verde and helped out mulching around trees. I met the other volunteers and understood a bit more about the project which is actually really cool. They are trying to grow vanilla here as it likes to grow on trees, of which there's loads here! and it's a very profitable crop. The only catch is that it's going to take one year and a half before they can harvest. If successful though, the project will be self-sustainable and able to employ people properly.

14.03.21

Yesterday I rented the cabaña! I'm so happy! I'm going to stay here for a bit longer.

Pulga has connected me with a wildlife conservation project, so I am not going anywhere! I'm also hanging out at project Sol y Verde more often. Last night we had a small party in the jungle.

Moreover, I got a job serving tables at the pizza shack, owned by Roberto, an Italian pizzaiolo. I did my first shift last night, before going to the party. I was clearing dust like a real local: When you come to these places completely covered in dust, you see people endlessly brushing yet endlessly enveloped in dust. The shift went ok, I served a couple of tourists, a family with 4 lovely children and a young guy who wanted to practice his Italian. I earned 45 quetzals, nothing really, but it was something to do and a way of meeting the locals.

Sitting at Mon Ami, surrounded so clearly by Jungle but looking across the water to the opposite shore and hills, I am reminded of Wales a lot, since from far away all you see is green but you can't make out the lush jungle, and you think you are looking at gentle, green hills, just like in Wales. Especially when it's cloudy, and the lake is silver, I get this impression. I told this to Santiago, Mon Ami's French owner, he responded that looking at the other side never reminded him of Europe. But I think that probably now I pointed it out, he's going to be reminded of it!

So, it's my last night at Mon Ami'. I can't wait to move to my new place, although I have really enjoyed it here. I loved the dorm, sleeping in the trees, watching the black squirrels, the birds and the lake from high up. Pancakes, fruit and honey for breakfast was also a favourite of mine. I guess from my new place I will still able to hear the next-door turkey gobbling like an old lady chuckling away an infectious laugh. It cracks me up every time.

15.03.21

I have just moved to my new home! I think I'll be happy here; I just have to move a few things around of course.

The other day, at the bonfire, Balta, Sol y Verde 's manager, was telling me about deforestation. The very next day I went to Flores, and I noticed how differently I see the landscape now, after Balta's chat. All the cattle ranches, which used to look so picturesque, now look likes scars on the land, big patches painful to see. You realise here, because of the contrast with the lush vegetation of the jungle, of the obscenity of it, the farmed land almost gets the quality of exposed raw flash. As I said, I almost felt physical pain as I looked at the landscape through the windscreen.

16.03.21

Generally speaking, here the moon often rises from the bottom up, not like in Europe where it rises mostly sideways. Last night the moon was huge, just a very thin slither of it, and deep red, it looked like a huge bright red Cheshire-cat smile in the middle of the black sky.

This morning I went to the Palomino pier early for yoga and the howler monkeys were very vocal in the trees right opposite me, so we did class together, which was awesome. The lake was beautiful and still and the colour was amazing. It's getting really hot now and it was lovely to swim in the lake early, but I know, I say that every day!

A funny thing that I have noticed yesterday, most people here seem to know I am working in the pizza place. Even people I've never met before.

19.03.21

I spent two days at Laguna Del Tigre, deep in the jungle, almost at the border with Mexico. It's been a great experience; as we were driving deeper into it, the pick-up truck struggling on many occasions in the deep tracks left by previous vehicles, I got this feeling of being in a place not often visited. Indeed, I went with a team of biologists doing research and monitoring jaguars and other wild animals, therefore this huge area is mostly visited only by them. Ronnie and Claudia, the two biologists, drove me there in their 4x4. We were followed by a film crew doing a documentary on the project and when we finally got to the camp, six hours later, we were greeted by technicians Pedro and Vitalino, who stay at the camp permanently on weekly shifts, alternating with others. There were howler Monkeys and spider ones, colonies of ants drawing on the jungle floor desire lines so massive, I thought they were trails left by a large snake. We changed camera traps and checked the footage. A Jaguar, amongst other animals, had visited the site in February. I recorded some jungle sounds, and I finally got really nice recordings of howler monkeys close up! The vegetation was incredible, lush, and at huge scale, roots came out of the ground supporting majestic trees covered in crawling foliage of all shapes and sizes. A display of real competition for light, and life. But at night, that's when things got magical. Fireflies danced at eyelevel and I have never seen so many stars in my life. The whole sky was covered, as far as my eyes could see. I don't think I've ever seen that before! I went to bed down in my tent and there was something crawling on the outside but it was hot so I ended up sleeping with the tent completely open and my head almost outside of it. Remarkably, I was not attacked by creepy crawlies in the night. The whole experience was so big really, that's almost lost on me, I was really privileged to be able to visit such a location.

PATRICK'S HUT

HUT EXTERIOR

24.03.21

 Today, the mother of all rains. I was at the project at the time so Theresa, the Check volunteer, and myself took refuge chatting upstairs in the wooden shack sitting on mats and watched the rain chucking it down on the forest trees, pretty awesome spectacle. We saw a huge beetle too, the size of a hand! After the rain, I went for a walk and saw toucans for the first time, with their beautiful beaks and distinctive call, flying through the trees! After the rain it became extremely hot, and it will be all week.

I have been teaching English to Rodrigo, my landlady's nephew, and also, I have been helping at the project, which has been nice. It's been an "all-girls thing" as the boys went to Rio Dulce for the week so now it's "clean and tidy" and I've been spending the very hot hours of the day there, chilling out, drinking iced oatdrinks and helping out on the farm. I have been raking some of the paths, including the one that goes up to the Mayan burial ground. New volunteers are coming and it's really nice to hang out there. Today Jinnie gave me a herbal infusion to put on my legs, which are totally itching all the time and full of bleeding bites, it's not even funny anymore. The stuff really helped, so she gave me some plants to take home and boil. I made the potion, but after applying it, I'm not getting the same relief at all. In fact, I'm still hitching. I wonder whether she gave me the right plants.

My landlady, Vilma, told me I can use the bicycle! I took it for a spin, it has no brakes, so I have to push it down the hill because the path is full of holes and stones, and you can get a little too much speed to go down it safely with no brakes. I am very grateful to have the bike.

I went shopping into town and on the way back I saw Jinnie's bike at the pier of "Doña Tonita", so I stopped to watch the sunset with her and Lottie, one of the new volunteers from the States. Betto, a local guy, was also there with some friends and his big dog Maya so we all shared a couple of beers. Then I rode home. It is really great having the bike to ride around El Remate, I hope I get to use it often.

One thing I haven't mentioned yet, there are loads of women, even very young ones, driving motorbikes and scooters. This is fantastic to see. Although the macho culture is very strong, and the ladies riding bikes is a reality only born out of necessity and convenience, it looks pretty forward thinking.

I haven't been to the city yet, but almost all the women I met don't wear make-up.

25/03/21

Today it must be the hottest day! I dip in and out of the lake for coolness, but it doesn't really help.

On another note, I have not eaten bread for two months. That's a record!

27/03/21

Doña Tonita, the actual woman, not the restaurant, saved my life two days ago. I went to the bar for a beer and Doña herself was serving. We got talking and she told me to put luke warm salty water on my bites, which she also said are ants' bites. She was damn right! The water really helps with the itching. I also understood that every day, I had been sitting in a particular spot in the garden where ants were eating me alive without me realising it!! I stopped sitting there. As a result, I am improving fast and today was almost pain-free.

Yesterday I also taught class to three kids, learnt some Spanish words while they learnt English ones. They were very cute.

26/03/21

The sky over the lake reminds me of the Simpsons clouds, today is no exception. I went to the Palomino pier early, had a lovely yoga session as there was a breeze! I even had some kind of yogic revelation about the mind and the self. It was weird and exhilarating at once. I started with a very crowded, busy mind, particularly so, but ended up in a lovely place. Theresa and Jinnie joined at some point, we had a chat and a few lovely swims. When they left, I stayed on a bit more, playing the harmonica. I am loving this new routine, also because I feel relaxed enough to play here. I've now played a little bit for 3-4 consecutive days and I'm starting to understand the harmonica a bit more, therefore I'm starting to enjoy playing it.

Drama in El Remate today! A guy almost drowned in the lake as he was drunk. I spoke to the guy who saved him. He had to pick him up from the bottom of the lake. The boy who almost drowned was taken to the hospital and we don't know how he is, but hopefully he's fine.

Later, on my way home, a man had a bike accident and smashed his face in. The accident was dealt "in house". I kept saying "call an ambulance, call the police" and I was met with incredulous eyes. That made me think about how much life here is different from the one I know, God knows how long it would take to get an ambulance out here. Anyway, the guy stood up by himself, and everyone was trying to help him. He looked like he wasn't feeling a thing because he was pretty drunk, but I am sure tomorrow it's going to hurt big time!

29/03/21

HUT INTERIOR

30/03/21

Oh, the little things of life make me happy these days! I am thrilled that the massive table that was in my room has finally been removed by my landlady! I am literally over the moon about it! I omitted it from the picture I drew yesterday but it was there, and it was huge.

I love going to the Palomino muelle in the morning. The flowers of the Lily pads are closed in the morning as I approach to do my morning yoga session; when I leave, a couple of hours later, they are fully open and stretched out in the sun. I find it very fitting and in tune with the universe, and a visual reminder of what I've just been doing, slowly and gently waking my body up and stretching it through my morning practice. It is also a reminder that we are one, it makes me feel part of this whole cosmic experience.

The new volunteer of Sol y Verde from the UK, Henry, joined this morning's yoga session. His practice is a bit too strong for my liking as it makes the whole pier shake. I will have to do my balances first thing, before he comes!

Tonight, Jinnie made pizza in the jungle, it was a joint effort, of course, as this is not a normal kitchen. But the pizzas were great and the sauce too! Seasoned with the herbs from their own allotment.

01.04.21

Today I found out that almost all my money has been stolen on-line. It was a hell of a shock: over 5 days, about 100 transactions buying stuff in one UK store had been made from my bank account, and by the time I noticed, almost all my money was gone! Whilst I am on the other side of the planet!

I had to spend almost 2 hours on the phone to the bank in the heat, but eventually and thankfully, it got sorted. Because of it, I missed a techno party that was banging somewhere really close, and I was hoping to find. Instead, I was stuck in a queue, listening to terrible muzak all morning! Then I went to Sol y Verde to plant some papaya plants and chat to Balta. It was a good afternoon. Afterwards, I went to play the harmonica and watch the sunset at Alice's pier. There were loads of turtles and fish swimming and feeding in the lake. I spent one hour looking at them and playing a soundtrack to their movements. I love this muelle and I also love swimming here. Every muelle is different. This one is surrounded by vegetation and you have to swim through it to get to the open water. It's a bit scary, of course, due to the possibility of crocodiles but I'm getting better with it. Now it is not scarier than generally swimming here, in the open. And actually, I love the little fear that you have to control as you swim through the reeds. At eye level, there are dragonflies, who are sometimes perched on the reeds. Here they are a beautiful bright shocking blue.

03.04.21

My landlady organised for the padlock on the second door of my hut to be cut, so now I can open a whole wall of my house. I am very happy! Not long after, a hummingbird flew in the house (the beauty of being able to open both doors and let the garden in). The poor thing was getting stressed and smashing in the net that creates part of the wall. So, I had to help it, I tried with a bright flower, but nothing. In the end I used the broom to guide it out. It worked! How cool though, it was in this room for a while.

3.4.21 – HUT INTEROR 2

I just found out the guy that drowned didn't make it. My thoughts are with his family and friends.

04.04.21

I woke up with the shits, last night I had a fried empanada with local spinach and cheese at Gardenia, which is usually really nice. But it was a bit late, and they rushed it. Or maybe I shouldn't have had fried food. Anyway, the hammock I have here in my room came into its own so I could laze about on it on this overcast lazy Easter Sunday. The hammock is exactly what I was missing at Mon Ami, when I was ill. This is the scenario I was preparing for, coming here. Luckily, it's not boiling hot today, therefore it is really pleasurable to lie here on the hammock… I don't even have the fan on today, imagine that!

06.04.21

Both my parents had the first jab of the AstraZeneca vaccine, they are both fine, thank God. Tomorrow I'll finally be able to break the news to them that I'm not going back to Europe at the end of the month. I didn't want them to worry about this change of plans until they had the vaccine.

Last night we had a lovely party at the project because today Jinnie is leaving, that's sad, the end of an era, after 5 months living here. I even played the guitar for a minute! After six weeks of abstinence!!! That was nice. Of course, I stopped as soon as someone noticed I was playing.

I don't think I've mentioned this already, but El Remate is definitely a richer town, they have two-ply toilet paper here!

07.04.21

Finally, I was able to tell mum and dad that I'm staying for longer. They weren't overjoyed, especially dad.

Jockey and Doggy had a huge fight today and it took ages to separate them. Doggy, my landlady's dog, has come out worst and I wonder whether I've upset the balance between these two dogs. They had scuffles before, but apparently nothing like this last fight. Both dogs love me, jockey likes to take walks with me, and doggy likes to be patted (Dogs don't get loads of cuddles here, they are more or less left wild). So, he likes the "European" attention.

Today our gate was open and, I wasn't there for the very start of the fight, but they ferociously went for each other, biting ears, neck, snout. It was pretty bad. I don't know if doggy needs a vet and I don't know if they would take him there anyway, poor Doggy, we will have to wait and see.

Last night I was visited by a huge green insect, a flying sort of giant cricket. He came for dinner, as there was a large insect flying by the light and getting stuck there.

09.04.21

I saw a, probably venomous, snake on the muelle yesterday, and today a big iguana came to say hello and hung out outside my hut for a while whilst I ate my lunch. After a couple of days of not feeling like swimming, I had a beautiful swim. There has been a very nice vibe on Alice's Muelle for the last couple of days, I met some new people that usually hang out at Alice's and a nice family that lives on the fish farm project round the corner.

10.04.21

VILMA'S PLANTS 10.04.21

12.04.21 KITCHEN CORNER

12.04.21

These are my last few days at El Ramate. The lake is beautiful and almost always all to myself. I escape the heat on Alice's pier every day and I am slowly getting around the idea of moving on and starting to get organised, which is as hard as getting organised to leave El Paredon. It feels like an impossible task but I'm going to try. I'm starting to get excited about moving on, which should give me some energy to enquire about transport. I'm really excited because I've decided to go to Mexico!!!

Over the last few days Rodrigo's mum baked me a lovely carrot cake and Doña Vilma and I have been sharing various fruits, including a huge spiky fruit that was about to kill me when it fell from the tall tree, really close to me. Doggy is healing very well. To cure him, they are using some jungle leaves with medicinal properties which they boil before applying it to the affected areas. Silly me, thinking they needed a vet to sort it out, when these people have a deep knowledge of medicinal plants!

15.04.21

I left El Remate! Unbelievable, and also sad. Last night there was one of the best sunsets ever. I left the house, and the whole road was reflecting a bright orange. I got to the lake, it was half blue and half orange, reflecting the sky, just amazing. I have never seen anything like it! I got into town and had a tea with Beto. It was his birthday, and he was high on acid and still mesmerised by the mega sunset he had just witnessed with his mates. On acid it must've been even more incredible.

Then I went to Elvia's Comedor as it was her birthday as well has her son's Lander. She is 40. I stayed for a bit and went to say goodbye to the guys in the taco place. There were a few people there and we had a nice chat. I bumped into some of the kids from the English class and didn't have the words in Spanish to say I was sorry I was leaving them. Early this morning, I was still saying goodbye to people as I was waiting for the bus. El Remate has been very good to me, everyone was lovely. It was particularly sad to say goodbye to my adopted family at Piazza, my home. Anyway, all things must end and now I'm sitting in a hammock on a mini-island in the middle of Rio Dulce, like something out of the Pirates of the Caribbean (we are indeed quite close to the sea now). 40 families live here, most of them are related, it is very peaceful, steeped in jungle, tiny wooden boats made out of one piece of wood gliding past. They are very cute. I met a little boy from the next island, Wilson. He told me his mum works away and he lives with his uncle. There are two tombstones here on this island, of a young man and an older one, the inscription says they both worked hard for the community. They died on the same day. Clearly this place has seen loads of political violence, and it's becoming more apparent. Today, whilst on the bus coming here, there was an advert of a forensic lab playing a few times on the local radio. The ad was matter of factly announcing that if any of your family had disappeared in 1970 or in 2016, they would be able to identify your relative!

The journey on the bus was nice. Suddenly looking slightly Thai, with jagged steep hills covered in trees sticking out of the ground. Then it got more "rainforest" and when in Rio Dulce I boarded the Lancha, well, that was a charming journey on the river! I'm getting excited to be close to the sea again, at some point I thought I could smell it. Also, pelicans and other sea birds are back. The mangrove is different here with full large trees coming out of the water. The architecture looks a bit more Caribbean. I saw a huge, amazing looking spider (not hairy) on an intricate web, and what I think was a baby iguana, as it was really tiny. But it could've been a lizard, and I saw bats.

There is a lovely muelle here where I think I'll be able to do some nice yoga tomorrow, and another lagoon on the other side of the island, with Lily pads with what seems to be huge pink flowers (they were closed, I'll have to investigate in the morning). On the next island they are noisy, will I be able to get a nice recording of this place later? I hope so as I'm not planning to stay more than one day now, as there is totally no signal here and unfortunately right now, I really need a connection to decide where to go next and more importantly how.

Today I didn't swim because I was still getting adjusted to everything. On this occasion, it took a lot of energy and used up all my confidence. All the confidence one needs to enter a new Guatemalan body of water. Especially because lady Philomena, although she knew I was coming, had nothing ready, the bed in the room wasn't made up, she had no food prepared (and didn't have anything vegetarian at hand – veg is coming later by boat so I'll have to wait until dinner time), even the water is not working yet, so I couldn't shower and I'm still sticky.
Nonetheless, I didn't have the energy to jump in the river which, FYI, is warm, I did stick my feet in it at least.

17.04.21

Last night I dined with with Philomena and her brother in their kitchen. I discovered that unfortunately the only boat leaving for the mainland was going to leave at 7 am, so I had to leave the island less than 24 hours after arriving, which was a shame. This entire experience has been a bit of a shock but a very short lived one.

The lancha sped up on the water in the early morning light, what an enchanting boat ride again, through gorges and lush vegetation coming all the way in the water, dotted with colourful houses on stilts, wildlife bathing, small wooden boats powered by one wooden ore. Women and children driving them with the confidence which in Europe is usually only of grown men. I got to the colourful Garifuna town of Livingstone by 8 am. Ancestors of my friend Vernon came here from St. Vincent, giving this town a Caribbean feel. The colours and street art made me think of Brixton, but by the sea. There are loads of Afro-Caribbean people about, but they all speak Spanish, not English or Patwa like in Brixton, which is quite amusing to me. Once I found a hospedaje, I went to explore the town and of course I hit the beach. I took a tuk-tuk just out of town, then I had a lovely walk on the beach (unfortunately it was quite littered with plastic), and I had my first taste of Caribbean Sea. I swam very close to pelicans and they are just gorgeous. In the evening I bumped into Natalie and Dimitri. They own Alice, the eco hotel in El Remate! They came from there by car with Cecile, their friend. We finally had a chance to spend some time together, as it never quite happened at El Remate! We had a couple of drinks in a crazy place by the beach where Tiffany and Stephanie, a Garifuna lesbian couple, were celebrating a birthday. Crazy ladies, crazy vibes, Tiffany even started to play the Jambe'. Definitely the vibe here is a lot more fiesta!

Nice to see Caribbean people here. It reminds me of why I like London, with the different cultures mixing, and funny how, the faces here are so familiar to me since there are many people from St. Vincent in London. Also, it is so good to be by the sea again, and the Caribbean Sea at that! With coastlines lined with palm trees, bananas and other lush vegetation.

Although at the place where I am staying, I'm having the dorm all to myself at the moment, I'm going to move to where the others are staying, Casa Rosada, because they have a muelle and the dorm is basically a huge veranda overlooking the pier. It is a fantastic room and I imagine that dawn from there should be amazing tomorrow.

I'm still in two minds about how to end my Guatemalan adventure and which way to enter Mexico, but if I decide to go to Antigua, hopefully the guys will give me a lift.

18.04.21

This morning, after a great awakening in the veranda, and a gorgeous banana pancake breakfast, Dimitri, Natalie, Cecile and I step off the muelle and set off on a lancha. They are giving me a lift to Antigua! Saving me a trip which would involve various bus changes. The journey on the river is just as beautiful as on the way down. It would have been nice to stay here a bit longer, but I went for the easy option and got the lift with the guys.

As my mind races through thoughts just like the lancha on the water, I realise, not for the first time on this trip, that my mind can run away with itself even here, where I am supposed to be living in the moment. Sometimes, at home, when trying to relax the mind, I spend time visualising locations such as this river or empty beaches and so forth, thinking that if I were in such places, my mind would be at rest. Now I am here, and yet, my mind spins off! I have noticed this more than once on this trip, which is making me think, maybe I'm starting to understand something deeper.

Anyway, the guys have their car waiting at Rio Dulce so it's a comfy pleasurable drive all the way to Antigua, chatting and listening to some nice music (finally, some indie music!). They saved me a much longer journey on three buses, and it's been nice to finally get to know them and spend some time with them. I am not sure Natalie is particularly happy I came along but there you go, I did.

This is a new route for me, through very dry land. Here big cacti stick out every now and then amongst shrubs and trees. Even if we are quite high up. I wonder if it's always like that, or if it's so dry because it's summer. The scenery is good, we pass small busy towns, gorges and rivers where people are spending their Sunday swimming, cooling and sharing food. Then we rise up into the now familiar landscape surrounding Guatemala City and Antigua. Good bit of driving, we get no traffic at all in Guate which is amazing. I go back to Casa Gitana. Carlos is making improvements on the place all the time and the garden looks as gorgeous as ever, if not more. As I arrive, the floor is covered in blue and purple petals, a lush Bougainville branch is dangling all the way to the floor as we turn the corner to get to the rooms; I ask about Cleto, Carlos tells me he died less than a month ago. How sad, he almost managed to sell the property and perhaps return to Italy, but it wasn't to be. He was so awfully ill. Carlos found him still alive, but covered in vomit and later he died in hospital. Poor Carlos. poor Cleto. It is extraordinary to me that I have been here so long I actually know someone that died (to be fair, he was almost dead when I met him and I always wondered how long he had left, now I know, 22nd of March was his expiry date. He died three weeks after I last saw him).

I have made good friends here and I care about them. Yesterday, Doña Vilma, my landlady in El Remate, tried to find me on Facebook and texted me on WhatsApp to make sure I was well. I went to get some food in town and I bumped into crazy Paris Milk, the cross dresser I met in El Paredon. He was with his mates, so we ended up drinking in the back of a restaurant (Covid restrictions mean it's illegal to drink at this hour, 6 pm) so this pizza joint turned into a speakeasy. It's one of their friends 30th birthday so we had a few drinks, they are a really nice crowd! They are Buena onda, as they say around here. Then I went home. As I sit here writing, right outside the room where Cleto died only a few weeks ago, I think of him and of death.

MY OLD ROOM AT CASA GITANA

19.04.21

Strange to fall asleep in Antigua without the jungle sounds to lull me into sleep. I am not going to lie, I was looking forward to spending one week without being eaten alive by various bugs and itching all over. At times the itching almost sends you up the walls, especially in the heat, and it's tiring, the skin is burning and in pain. Still, I love the jungle, next time I'm going to try and use some repellent. The bites of El Remate were something else. Let's see what Mexico has got to offer as far as that's concerned.

20/04/21

I am back in San Pedro for some more Spanish classes. It's a totally different vibe this time. It's grey and thunder-stormy with beautiful lightning. I have a fantastic room which is basically one huge window on the lake. Very happy. The huge window is a sort of wooden trap door on the wall, which you can open so that you can sit right out. I've picked the top bunk, so when I lie there, it feels like I'm lying right on the water. This place, Cristallina, is cool: there is a wooden pier outside and, in the lounge, it has these huge wooden windows that come down, like the one in my room, so it's perfect now that the weather is not great, because it's a lot more sheltered than other places. It has it all! My room also feels so detached from everywhere else in the building, I've even felt happy to play the harmonica for a while, just looking out at the lake.

21.04.21

Today after class I went to San Juan, following the lake bank, climbing over the rocks on the side of the mountain, and then into the vegetation, some proper mountain goat-ing. Luckily, at the most difficult bit, I met some people going the opposite way and they gave me a hand, literally. The water looked so blue and inviting, but I pressed on. From the steep hill I climbed, I reached the road and then I was there. What a lovely, colourful town. Very Indigenous. Its main focus is textile, and it has many shops selling indigenous garments and crafts. The streets are covered in murals and the main street was adorned with wonderful straw hats of different shapes attached to ropes on opposite buildings and creating a lovely covering over the road. Some of the hats had been hand-painted as well, so if you looked up, you saw some designs. I continued to the beach called Cristallina and on the way, I passed another beach. I wasn't able to find its name, but this turned out to be way more exciting than Cristallina, in my view. Or maybe, as today was stormy, Cristallina was not at its best. Who knows. The name suggests clear waters, but today, the lake looked like the sea, with proper waves and the beach unfortunately was quite dirty with plastic. The beach is long though and I can imagine it's lovely on a fine day. You are closely surrounded by steep mountains and volcanoes behind you, and you get to see quite a lot of the lake and the layers of volcanoes and mountains on the other side. The other, nameless beach however, has two rows of dead trees firmly sticking out of the water, quite close to the beach, and more huge dead trunk bases with showing roots uprooted on the beach. Behind you, the strip of land that goes up to the road, is farmed all the way to the beach with cauliflowers, bananas, other veg and corn. I sat facing the waves and played my harmonica for a bit. Here, for the first time, I felt like I could belt it out a bit, because there was no one around and the waves were quite loud. Then I walked through the tall corn to get back to the town and the muelle. The boat trip back was fun as the lake was really choppy! Who would've thought that the water of a lake could get so rough! In the evening I went for a lovely soup in a café with a fantastic library of books, mostly good books, in different languages. The owner was very nice, and we chatted as I ate. Her dog is called Gigi because she likes Buffon the ex-goalkeeper of Juventus!

Today, chatting to my teacher, I realised that so far, I hadn't really understood the many layers of politics, life and the differences between the people. It might sound obvious, but the indigenous are disadvantaged compared to the Latinos. So, I guess most people I met from the city, which so much resemble middle-class people from all over the world, were actually Latinos. To think of it, probably most local hostel owners were Latino in El Remate. not indigenous.

27/04/21

Today is a very happy day. I was meant to fly home (imagine that!) And instead, I changed my ticket. It's now official, I'm leaving on the 31st of July. From Mexico. Now I just have to get there on Saturday.

This afternoon I went for a walk as I had a lot of homework and I needed to space it out a bit. I walked about San Pedro and, don't ask me how, I got to a bit I've never been before. I went over the first tongue of land that goes out onto the lake, to find myself on a large beach. Here the whole lake opens up in front of you, you can even see the mountain peak that inspired the book "Little Prince". How very peaceful. A few local people were swimming, washing themselves or their clothes, the birds were chirping, and it was amplified by the mountains (I still don't have a recording of San Pedro, and tomorrow I'm leaving).

The lake has risen in recent years and there are abandoned houses foundations sticking out of the water. It is like another world... I wonder if this beach was the Fincha after all, although I seemed to arrive to it too quickly and suddenly.

On the way back I stumbled upon some streets with very funky bars I've never seen before. I have a very rough idea of where I actually was at this point. How cool though. It was like visiting a completely new place and again, it made me think that here I could've spent longer to really get under the skin of San Pedro. Altogether I spent almost 2 weeks here, but not in one go, so it took a while to get back into it the second time.

23.04.21

This morning I had my last lesson and had to say goodbye to Letty, my teacher and San Pedro. I took the boat to Panacachel, on the other side of the lake. I found a basic but lovely room very close to the pier, where the owners are a very sweet couple and have a courtyard full of gorgeous plants. The green finger is his and her name is Rosa; she couldn't have been called in any other way!

Pana is "huge", compared to where I have been lately, it feels a bit like being in America, I don't know why, maybe because the streets are slightly larger, but then many people are dressed in local clothes. There is a long promenade, many piers, and a large beach. It's all a bit much really, a bit intense for me, but I'm here to meet Stephanie and go to Mexico tomorrow! I spend the day exploring, it's very touristic. The promenade is lined with restaurant with, would you believe it, waiters in uniform, standing outside and trying to entice people in with the menu in their hands. I hadn't seen scenes like these in a very long time and it's the first time I see this here in Guatemala.

24.04.21

Last night I met up with Stephanie. She was good, as always. We went to a place where they make these gorgeous drinks. You tell them which spirit you prefer and whether you fancy a sweet or a sour drink. Then this beautiful, always different drink is produced and presented to you.

This morning early, I left for Mexico driving in the clouds over lake Atitlan. I was thinking that I've been seeing so many Vesuvius, the landscape is dotted with them. Guatemala has many steep hills covered in green and most have the same or very similar shape to Vesuvius. I considered my time in Guatemala has ended. What a great experience. I made friends, I loved the sunsets, landscapes and every moment. I don't really want to leave. But I must.

I crossed the border with 30 rolled joints, no problem, although a bit scary, but I figured out that a tourist bus was not going to get stopped so I chanced it. It didn't help that all the songs playing on the radio in the shuttle bus were about criminals and people getting banged up. When I thought I got away with it, the coach turned into a road leading to a checkpoint. I shat my pants; I'm not going to lie. Luckily, it was just the way we had to go; the checkpoint was not operational.

As soon as we crossed the border, a big expanse, the peaks covered in pines of Guatemala gave way to valleys and ranchos and dry skinny trees. Oh, I wish I knew the names of all the plants. Everything is vast: huge boulders, suddenly everything feels chunky and north American. A weight lifted off my shoulders. I guess I'm slightly claustrophobic when it comes to tall, thickly packed mountains. I had the same feeling on the Scottish Isles, where you seem to be always surrounded by peaks. As soon as we got into Mexico, and everything opened up, so did I. After 12 hours, (we took ages at passport control) we arrived at San Cristobal de La casa.

It looks like I booked a really chilled out hostel, where everyone plays an instrument, and anything goes. It's busy though, and so is this town. San Cristobal is very beautiful. It looks like a slightly more modern version of Antigua, but buzzing, like Covid never existed! On first impression it's really cool, but I am suffering from a little culture shock and it feels a bit intense and intimidating, with all those hip people. I hope it's not going to be a pretentious town. Everyone plays music, carries an instrument, has crazy hair. Apparently, there is even going to be a Techno party tonight, I'm clearly overwhelmed! I go to dinner in a place where a band is playing. A guitarist, a girl sings and plays the cajon and another plays an accordion. After a while I get into it. Then I go for a stroll, but the streets are very busy so for tonight I'm cutting out early.

25.04.21

I slept really well on my top bunk, but there's loads of us in this dorm because two couples are sharing a single bed. A Covid fest? We'll see.

It reminds me of Apulia here, in the garden there are trees that resemble almond trees. There is a nice rooftop where one can do yoga in the morning, so I hope I can get used to the crowds and stick it out for a bit. Or shall I come back here for a week or two a bit later on as I travel between the two coasts? Right now, I'm thinking I might cross the country twice, mainly because I've heard that July can be quite rainy on the coast... I am tired, but I should really check transport etc. to get an idea on how to do this trip.

Well, on first impression, and compared to fifteen years ago when I came here last, Mexico is a much richer place now, and a lot richer than Guatemala.

Oh man, the food is going to be nice. Today I had some tortillas, so fine. And finally, I discovered what I am supposed to do with the cream usually served with the breakfast, this time it was splashed all over the egg. My breakfast was a pig fest. I didn't quite realise what I was ordering and I got a plate with two eggs on top of tortillas with the cream, plantains, beans and an extra 10 tortillas on the side (of course I didn't eat all of them).

Just like Antigua, San Cristobal de La casa has a mirador, with a nice pine forest around it where you can keep cool. It's bigger than the one in Antigua. I found a hidden spot and played some harmonica. I felt better. I got it out of my system. At the hostel there are guitars, so tempting.

Last night I fell asleep even before finding out where the techno party was and today I found out I actually knew someone there because I bumped into Jann, the French botanist that I met at project Sol y Verde in El Remate and he told me he went to the party.

26.04.21

I went to the canyon Sumidero just outside San Cristobal and I saw a couple of big crocodiles. They were so immobile they looked fake and I almost stretched my hand to touch them. Amazing creatures. I didn't like the first bit, when they took us to the sanctuary and they encouraged people to pat the baby crocs and play with the boa constrictor. Of course, I didn't. The lancha trip on the river was striking sheer drops either side, very different from the rivers in Guatemala with the mangrove. We got to the highest point, the guide told us that in this very spot, Indigenous people jumped to their death rather than become slaves to the conquistadores. It was mighty high and beautiful, and, I don't know if it's true, but I started to think about all those people at the bottom of the river.

There were pelicans too, but we were quite far away from the sea. Then I returned to the hostel and hang out with the others there. This hostel is so laid-back with lots of cool art on the walls and full of crazy people but muy buena onda. I met a very nice girl, Mariana, from Uruguay.

I went out to dinner and got lost in San Cristobal. What a nice town, there is a huge market, full of amazing veg and fruit, all the buildings are colourful and there's loads of narrow lanes, music and art everywhere, the food is great, lots of young people. I am really starting to enjoy it but I am leaving tomorrow, I got my ticket. It's okay, it's best to come back here with a plan! or with friends. So, I'm cool to go, I think.

27.04.21

This morning I did some yoga on the roof. The city soundscape was so different! Anyway, being up there reminded me of my childhood home, where the roof was covered in tarmac like this one is. Every time I'm on such roofs, I get transported back in time to when I was playing up there with my brother, I see the iron spiral staircase going up to the roof-terrace, with the mezzanine half way up with the pantry with a million food tins and my dad's blue, metal toolbox, which we decided, when I was three years old, that it would also be mine.

Later I went to Arbolito, a river with caves and a natural arch in a beautiful pinewood. I was able to play a bit by the water. It was lovely to spend the afternoon there. Going there was a lovely trip as well, in the collectivo, rising up above San Cristobal, nestled in the valley below. Everything around was dark green. The collectivo had an ingenious way to open and close the back door, where the driver had a rope attached to a lever to do it. I also noticed that people driving around selling gas have this wonderful system to advertise their presence.

A chain is attached at the back of the bumper, with two or three thick metal rings dangling from it and touching the floor making this really loud teeny beautiful distinctive sound on the cobbled streets.

Eavesdropping in San Cristobal, many people have very deep conversations about politics, philosophy and life. A far cry from your average conversations in most places.

A difference I have noticed with Guatemala is that in San Cristobal there are many toy stores laden with all kinds of toys. In Guatemala the choice was very limited (mind you, I have been to "desolate", smaller places).

I didn't buy a guitar today. I'm sure I'm going to regret it. Tonight, I will take the night bus, I'll be a bit sad to leave this very chilled hostel.

28/04/21

We travelled all night. A super full moon, first orange, then bright white, guided us and brightened up the night sky revealing huge valleys and the contour of the faraway mountains. We passed Tuxla. It looked huge, lights sprawling in all directions for miles. After taking a connection with a collectivo, I finally made it to Mazunte, hirteen hours or so later. I found a room on the beach, without really understanding anything of this place yet.

The beach is lovely with coffee colour sand and rocks in the water that remind me of the Goonies. We are on the Pacific Ocean. Water is clear and fresh, and I have a swim straight away. The town seems lovely: it has a river (dry at the moment, but I guess at different times water does run) And all these unpaved roads running along it, immerse in thick vegetation. The main road is paved. There are many yoga centres and bars. And turtles! I have to go on a tour as soon as possible.

In the late afternoon I go to play the harmonica at the very end of the beach, the ocean covering my screeches, therefore I am able to play happily for a while. The beach is certainly not deserted but it's cool. There are places to explore, walks to do and turtles to see! I think I'll stay a week.

I'm super excited as I've booked a turtle tour for tomorrow morning. I go for a walk about and there is a large group of dancers practicing to live drums in the Main Square.

29.04.21

I saw turtles! Dolphins and stingrays this morning. The turtles would poke their cute faces out every now and then and the dolphins would swim alongside the boat, even jumped a couple of times. Just magical. We swam in the open ocean with goggles, but the water was black and a bit scary, the current was strong and we could hear the dolphins communicating underwater. The coastline was also lovely, with all these little beaches, I saw Punta Cometa from the sea and another unspoiled beach. Later I'll go there for sunset. I think it will be a lovely walk.

30.04.21

Yes, the beach was untouched, wild, pretty empty and huge. Very atmospheric, with the waves crushing, the valley, palm trees and the mountains behind. I went all the way to the end, found a spot in the shade and practiced some harmonica nice and loud against the crashing waves.

In the evening there was a beach party. I was already asleep, and it woke me up, so I went to take a look. The moon was bright and shimmering over the water and the music was okay. I didn't want to drink so I just bopped for a bit, then went back to our restaurant/hut and had a chat with two other guests for a while. I had plans of waking up early and doing all these beautiful things this morning, but I woke up at 9:30, the latest I've ever woken up on this trip, and I don't seem to be able to make any decisions today. I have already been for a nice walk along the beach, hopefully a coffee will wake me up.

01.05.21

The ocean here is super powerful. Yesterday a girl had to be helped as she could not swim back. The sound is incredible too as huge waves crash onto the beach, sometimes they are 3 m high, I would say. At times a huge and unpredictable wave goes all the way up the beach sweeping things away with it (someone lost their phone). Dangerous.

I went to practice on the other beach, at the spot I found the other day, a small inlet in the rocks. The waves were so tall and strong and long it was amazing, but after a while I had to leave as some bigger waves were coming right up to the edge of where I was. I didn't know if the tide was coming in, was fully in or what, but it was clear to me that one wave a little bit bigger than the ones I was seeing, and I could have been easily swept away. It was a dangerous place. Therefore, I walked back a bit and played in a safer place. Clearly others couldn't hear me over the waves, so I didn't mind being closer to them. Then, I watched the sunset drinking a couple of beers; this beach is so wild and calm, it's the perfect place, really... If only you could swim here! But apparently the sea is always pretty rough. And there are sharks too, I've seen a sign.

In the evening I had dinner with Bill, an American guest at my hotel and Carlos, one of the staff. We went to a busy place that Carlo suggested and it was boiling. Earlier in the day Carlos walked out of his job because they accused him of stealing. They did find what they had misplaced, but by that point, Carlos was upset. Shame, because I think the family running the hotel are ok, a little rough around the edges, but fun. They also have four incredibly cute kittens!

I thought I was tanned, but I've noticed I now have the mark of my sandals on my feet. I've also finally lost my toenail today. It's better, so it doesn't hurt anymore every time a wave comes! It looks horrible of course.

I went to Puerto Escondido. Two buses and an hour later, I get to this quite ugly town, but the bay is actually stunning, pity for the boats moored and the buildings. It must've been amazing up to 10 years ago. You can swim here (unfortunately it is also where most boats are anchored), there is a lagune and a mangrove. They have hammocks in the trees. I relax on one of them for a while and an old couple offers me a mango. It's mango season, they are everywhere and delicious.   In Puerto Escondido there is a walk you can do on the rocks by the sea, they have created a path on the rocks with cement and steps. It goes around the point. I found a bit of it in the shade and practised for an hour watching the huge waves. Walking through town, I almost bought a guitar. Then I gave myself a very good excuse to postpone the purchase. I told myself that where I'm going next, they'll definitely have one I'll be able to borrow and promised myself I'll buy one when I get to the other coast, where there'll be no more travelling. But I seriously considered buying one for half an hour. I actually managed to step into the shop and even chatted to the lovely, old man running the place... I would've loved to buy the guitar from him. At least now I know what I'm going to get. A three-quarter guitar.

On the way back, I walked the main beach promenade of Puerto Escondido, which redeemed it a bit, as actually walking there was quite nice. I took the bus back, watching the dry countryside and the mango plantations through a playboy sticker on the bus window. I didn't know, but the mango fruit hangs from a long twig attached to a leafy branch. It's a pretty tree, wide, not too tall with lovely light green thin leaves. Most rivers were dry but two and, judging from the scenery it looks like it is going to be lovely at my next location, which is an hour drive north of Puerto Escondido...The other day, chatting to a woman in Mazunte, I found out that the river there is almost always dry. Apart from when it rains big time. Needless to say, she told me that 30 years ago, the river was always full.

I thought I was going to be badly affected by the loss of the toenail. But I can hardly care! like I'm not caring too much about the hair sometimes I have on my legs, and certainly not caring much about the ones under my armpits. An incredible achievement! I used to be so obsessed with these things!!

02.05.21

Here it's all about palm trees "smashing out" of roofs and floors (they build around the trees). Shame I haven't had a chance to draw it, like the garden at the hostel in San Cristobal, which also deserved a drawing!

Last night I watched a very good circus show in the main square of Mazunte. It was really nice, everyone was sitting on the floor, the kids joining in. The compere did say this was the first time everyone was together like this in a while.   Earlier in the day I learned that Mexican kids are still not going to school. So, everything is normal, more or less, open, apart from schools. And of course, we have to wear masks in public places. I am sorry to say, it's always the young French travellers who flaunt the rules more than anyone else and won't wear masks in enclosed places.

I went swimming this morning, on the right-hand side of the beach, where it is relatively safe. It is an incredible experience swimming in such powerful sea. You have to kind of dance with it, asses its every move like a boxer. In the silence it's just you and the ocean, you have to get lost and feel at one, it's a very "in the moment" experience. I am learning that the best time to swim is when the tide is all out.

Right outside the restaurant the waves are always very big and this morning the waiters were worrying the whole restaurant would be taken away by the sea because the waves were getting even stronger and advancing further and further up the beach.

In the afternoon the sea got calmer and I was having a lovely swim when I bumped into Welsh Hannah, the one travelling with Montana. She told me that generally the sea here is a lot calmer and these five days were an exception. That made me so happy! There is hope after all for me and the Pacific.
Hannah is with some friends, and they are stuck here because some other friend left with the keys to their van so they're waiting for the keys to be returned. Well, they are stuck three days at the beach, not bad, I can think of many worst places to get stuck in.

The most beautiful thing happened a little later. They were releasing baby turtles. So black and small against the tallest of waves. I can hardly describe the feeling, the immensity of the moment. The fact that they just know what to do, they were just born this morning and they were being released from inside coconut shells by various people and kids. They were smaller than the palm of my hand, but fearlessly they walked towards a shifting wall of powerful water.

03.05.21

Today is just perfect. The sea is beautiful, the beach is deserted, it is lunchtime and I already had three long swims. I was going to go away today, but it's just so gorgeous that by 11 am I had changed my mind three times, and, in the end, I went to pay for one extra night. Now I made the decision to stay, I can really relax and enjoy the rest of the day. I should learn something from this. It's happened time and time again on this trip.

The bay is gorgeous today. The rocks sticking out of the blue sea, white waves crashing onto them. The feature of the bay are the rocks, they look like triangles, many of them on the land, on Punta Cometa, on the far right there is a triangular rock, and this shape seems to be repeated in the water all the way to the other end of the bay. Very picturesque. It reminds me of colour recalling. Apparently having plants with the same colour in different parts of your garden is a very good way to create a pleasant visual experience, for your eye is drawn to different areas of the garden that are showing the same colour. Something like that. And the rocks here, with the repeating shape, and their scattered positioning in the water, make me think of that.

In Mazunte, and all over Mexico it is full of original VW beetles, at various stages of decay. The best one here is a smashed up, rusty white beetle with only one light and bits completely missing or falling off, driven around by a fearless white woman.

05.05.21

The last couple of nights have been moonless, the starry sky was amazing. I even saw two shooting stars. Then, finally, yesterday morning I left Mazunte and embarked on a four-hour journey to my next location by collectivo, taxi and boat, all very crowded. In the taxi ride it was six of us! I thought I was being lucky getting the front seat when someone else got in too! So, in the end, as I'm always the smallest, I got pushed to the edge of the seat, next to the gear stick and the driver was driving at speed on bendy roads. On the bus, I got sandwiched between two large men, and again, they both spilled over into my seat.

All in all, not a comfy journey. Eventually I got to the island of Chacahua, which is incredible. It is sea, waves, Laguna, no actual roads, cash machines or police, loads of animals and plants, it is in the national park, and everything happens on the beach in this small community. People look slightly different too. When I ask Carlos, the owner of my beach hut, he explains the people here are Afro Mexicans (indeed they look slightly African). The vibe is super chilled, and, if it's true that the restaurant in the square also sells pot, then I can stay here for a while! Right now, I have a lovely room on the first floor with a deliciously breezy outside space with two hammocks, table and chairs. I share this space with Flo, a tattoo artist from Germany who works without using a machine. Today she was inking a French girl called Mary. A Polish girl called Ivana also showed up and we all chatted for a while. Then I left them to it, to go for a swim.

06.05.21

It's true! the restaurant also sells huge bags of weed. I can relax now and possibly stay here for a while. Mind you, the grass is not very good...

Last night I went to the beach, and I bumped into two girls I had met in the morning, Bridget and Amy. Bridget was rather pissed on rum and coconut water, and she took me to the pot shop/restaurant. On the way there she told me she had been to Puerto Escondido all morning to transfer some money as she is buying a piece of land here on the beach. No wonder

she was celebrating. We had a few drinks with some other people too. On the beach there was a bonfire, they were doing a peyote ceremony. Alberto, one of the people I was with, was telling me I should do it, ask for Laura, she'd guide me through it. It was very tempting, especially because Bridget was telling me we should perhaps just go and sit around the fire and see what happens. If I stay here a bit longer, I will do it, but it was my first day on the island and I didn't want to lose my mind with complete strangers on day one. Bridget understood, she said she was like me too when she first arrived. She's been here a few months now, who knows, we may go to it next time.

Last night I also discovered that they don't put their clocks forwards in Chacahua, unlike the rest of Mexico, which explains why the other morning my phone was displaying 7 am but the sky looked like it was just dawning. I found that odd at the time.

This morning I asked Carlos to show me where to wash my clothes. They have a big container full of clean water you can collect with a smaller bowl to pour over the clothes. When I went to do this, I saw there was a small fish in the water! That made me laugh.

Around lunchtime I found a nice spot on the rocks on the right-hand side of the beach. There is a row of rocks that shelters the area from the waves, and it also limits the lagoon on the other side. It has a few trees on it, so I found a shaded spot and played the harmonica for a bit, watching the surfers. Then I went for a swim, and it was really hot. Later on, the sky got grey and the sea dark blue and then we had the most dramatic storm with lightning and thunder and bucketing rain. It was still going on, various hours later. As I saw it approach, I ran home to get the sound gear to record it, but frankly I missed it. I started to record the waves and the start of the storm, but the beach was still busy at this point. When it started to rain a bit more, I took refuge under a canopy on the beach, but there were other people there, obviously chatting. The storm got even stronger, and we all had to run and take refuge at the same restaurant. Now I was stuck there with the

noise of people, and this is when the storm really kicked in. It was not even 7 pm (Chacahua time) so I stalled ordering dinner.

When I finally made my mind up about eating, the restaurant staff were having their dinner, so I had to wait. When I eventually got my food, and I knew this would happen, there was a power cut too, so then I had a romantic dinner for

one, by candlelight. Until the wind blew the candle out, and it was actually nice to be plunged in darkness and then suddenly and intermittently see the lightning revealing the contour of the palm trees, battered by fat raindrops. When I finally made it home after dinner, the storm was still going strong, so I was hoping to go back and do some recording of it from there, but, as the power was not resumed, a loud generator kicked into action, so I gave it a miss. My usual luck! Well, it means I had time to write this, and enjoy this storm in the moment.

07/05/21

The island still has no electricity.

This morning, when I went for a walk on the beach, I met a man, and he showed me some marks on the beach and explained to me that the turtles had been on land to lay eggs. The eggs had already been removed, I hope by the resident volunteers, and not by people just wanting to eat them. I'm going to try and find this volunteer woman today.

I found the volunteer, he is a man, Mariano, and he tells me that now it's the end of the season and they don't do anything anymore, there are just the last few nests left to hatch in about a week, he says if I'm still here I can join him to release the baby turtles.

Back at the hut it is a lot quieter today, since there is no electricity, and the birdsong is just amazing. One of the few people able to work today is Flo, since she uses no electricity to make her tattoos.

After the rain, the ocean has calmed down and today the water is amazing. I spend all day on the beach swimming and in the evening I go for dinner with Bridget to the restaurant where I can also buy pot. We spend an interesting couple of hours with some locals, José and Cerille, also called Ciro. I sing to him the Neapolitan song with his name in it, he seems to know this song. Who knows.

08.05.21

Amy, Bridget and I went to the other side of the lagoon. Restaurant tables and hammocks are set up in the crystal-clear water, the sand is nice. Palm trees all around. the sea is so calm that the lagoon is meeting the sea seamlessly. We have lunch before exploring this side. We are in the national park now, the beach is really wild and beautiful, there is a natural arch too. A very beautiful day.

09.05.21

Carlos made me switch room, I now have a lovely hammock on the patio and a lovely view of the ocean! Balance has been restored. I also have a private bathroom! Not that I care about it, but I am being utterly spoilt. The sea has been just perfect once more. I hope it lasts. I am definitely staying three more days, but if it holds up, I may do the whole month!

10.05.21

It's Mother's Day here today and the excitement is palpable. All the mums are getting ready to be fussed, music blaring songs about mums, people organising parties. I reckon the whole town will be pissed by lunchtime. This should be interesting. Also, this morning I woke up to full gun shots. Some poor animals surely being sacrificed for the big day. I spent all day on the beach, every now and then returning to my hut and I could hear the mariachi playing in town. In the evening I went to bed only to wake up a couple of hours later. Since the party was still going on, I decided to go to it. There were in fact two parties, right next door to each other. One was a Mother's Day celebration, banging Mexican tunes through the loudspeakers. Next door, a birthday, full stage, lights, DJ, super loud. It was funny as they were right next door to each other, and everywhere else was quiet or shut. The whole town was attending and some of the foreigners too. I met Amy and Brigitte, we kept going between the two parties drinking margaritas and dancing to Latino music, (that was a first for me). It was a crazy night. People were drinking loads. We ended up at a bonfire on the beach where we met three guys and one of them started singing French and Italian songs accompanied by a tambourine. He could sing very well, knew all the songs and could speak a bit of both languages too.

11.05.21

Lazy day, obviously. I didn't go for my usual early morning walk, as I didn't wake up early enough for it. It was almost 8 am when I walked to the beach and the sun was strong behind a veil of cloud, the light was bright and hurting my eyes, so I couldn't really go for it. Maybe the margaritas had something to do with it too. I had my heart set on breakfast anyway, because last night, when I met Amy, she surprised me with unsweetened almond milk which she bought on the mainland and knew I was after. How nice of her! So indeed, I had a nice breakfast, I also got coffee and, basically, I'm definitely staying one more week (at least!).

I'm loving that the Internet is not really working so there is no point in looking at the phone. Today I spent the day swimming, watching the fish and the people through the crest of the waves, which I love. I lazed about in the hammock, had some tostadas with guacamole and mangoes for lunch. A real lazy day, I didn't even consider going for yoga at 10 am. Yesterday I met this French guy, Nicholas, who runs the holistic shack and does yoga every morning. I had told him I was going to join him today, but that was before the party. I am planning to have a much healthier day tomorrow but I met Bridget, and she told me there's another party tonight, so we'll see if tomorrow is the day I start my healthy routine!

Today the sea was great for both swimmers and surfers (it had been crap for surfers over the last four beautiful days) so there was a great sense of happiness all around the beach. Here there are many points where people can surf, with waves for all abilities and it's quite nice to sit and watch the surfers in different points of the horizon and at different skill levels.

This morning I was rather daydreaming on my first swim, the water was warm, and I just swam there for a while, when I snapped out of it and turned around, I was the furthest out I've ever been. I panicked a bit as today the sea is growing again, so there were lots of different currents. Panic is an exaggeration, but I thought, of all the days when I could've swum away, I chose today, when the sea is getting strong again. Well as I said, I was a bit slow this morning.

A day of reflection, funny how now, after a week, as I get used to things, I relax more and more into it. What I love about these places I've visited, is the unpredictability and the fact that you have to adapt. You may have some plans, only to find out that, for no reason all, the shops you're after are closed for three days, or there may be no electricity for half a week. So, you have to adapt your expectations all the time. And you do realise that there is no point in worrying about stuff. That's when you learn to go with the flow and that no tragedy is going to happened, which is the attitude of these places anyway.

12.05.21

On my usual morning walk I meet lots of crabs, big and small with bulging eyes. They can be extremely fast and very funny. The other day I passed by one and it opened up its arms in a kung-fu stance, ready to fight! So funny. I also noticed they can jump. The ones living on the rocks by the lagoon do jump between rocks. On my walks there are also many coconut shells, sometimes dead fish, even big ones, that then get eaten by the vultures. And every morning I notice that this beach is rather clean, even after parties on the beach, it's not too bad and you don't get loads of plastic being washed up. The best thing about the water though, is the temperature. Even my best friend Cristina would get in quickly, and she is notorious for stepping in the water really slowly.

I am walking further and further, today I got to the midpoint of the bay. It's very beautiful here, as it's very wild and quiet. I love to listen to the sound of waves, how sometimes there's almost no sound, and other times it is almost deafening. I love the pink/silvery light on the sea as the sun rises. Here the sun actually sets behind the beach, but you can still catch a great sunset because the sun sets on the lagoon (which reminds me a bit of El Remate, with muelles, big red setting sun, the quiet sound of almost still water). Where the Laguna meets the sea, there is a little beach that comes out into the water, which means you can sit "inside" the lagoon to watch the sunset. Pretty special. I have also discovered that the area where the rocks divide lagoon and sea, is the perfect location to spend that time of day, as it's free from mosquitoes, because of the sea breeze and, I suspect, also because amongst these rocks, live the bats. As the sun sets, they start flying out from the rocks beneath me to go hunting.

When I went to this spot in the evening, a mini disaster happened. My faithful companion, the harmonica, has a problem. One C does not play. What a bummer. Hope I can fix it. The sunset was incredible though.

Over dinner at a pop-up comedor in the sandy town square, I shared the table with a couple from Mexico City and their toddler. The man told me that A) Here it is really busy compared to how it normally is (and today I don't think it's busy) and B) five years ago there were only 5 or 6 Palapas on the beach, therefore Chacahua has already seen a massive "development". The man, Angel, is a health professional and tells me he is quite happy with how Mexico has managed the pandemic and he is happy it has reopened.

13.05.21

Was it a minor disaster that the C on the harmonica is gone? Or is it a chance for discovery? I am going to be forced to explore all the more complicated scales and intervals that don't use the C. A chance to explore more combinations. I woke up this morning thinking positively about it.

For today, I had also organised to go and help out on a new farm project, so I met up with Isai, from the vegetarian bar, and we went by bike to the farm. There is only one road on this Island, connecting the town at one end to the pier at the other and his property is 3/4 of the way up the bay. In pure Latino fashion our appointment was not early, then, we were late one hour leaving as Isai cooked some breakfast for us to take, and when we got there it was too hot to work. Fabiola, who also works at the veg bar was there with their dog. We had some beans and tortillas and mixed vegetables for breakfast and had a chance to talk a bit. They are from Puebla, close to Mexico City. Their land has almost nothing on it now, what they had planted didn't make it, so they plan to plant melons, pineapple, cucumber and other veg that can basically grow in sand. For the moment, they sleep in hammocks under a canopy where they also have a wood fire. They are building a wooden house (they have put into the ground only four small cement pillars) and everything else will be made from wood, and sustainable with the restaurant and camping. They have a lovely stretch of beach to look at. After breakfast, as it is too hot to work, they start snoozing in the hammocks. I decide it's best for me to head back, so I can go for a swim, here the sea is a little too rough, but of course, it's midday and they live perhaps more than an hour walk away from town. I go anyway hoping for a collectivo to pass by. In the blistering sun, I get a chance to look at this island where it is still wild. Behind the beach, there are cactus plants (maybe nopal) then the road and on the other side there are tall trees with foliage and palm trees. Lots of bird songs fill the sky. When I'm almost at boiling point, (I've only walked 20 minutes) and after two failed hitchhike attempts, a collectivo comes.

The sea is a little rough again, hence it is a little murky for all the sand being tossed about, but now (after having swum in it when it was calm and crystal-clear) I don't have a problem with it, it doesn't make me slightly uncomfortable as it did on week one. I'm happy to go in and swim and I know the water is actually extremely clear, hence you can see the sand swirling. Basically, now it looks sandy, rather than murky.

14.05.21

At 8 a.m. this morning Amy and I met Cerille the boatman, and we went for a tour of the lagoon in search of crocodiles. This lagoon is massive, there is mangrove, little islands, big lakes, many birds. Cerille talked about the four types of mangrove,

red, white, black and I can't remember the fourth one. He showed us how from the seed, on one side the root grows towards the water, on the other it makes a flower. On our way back we saw a large crocodile swimming in the middle of the lagoon. When we tried to get closer for a second time, the engine noise scared him, and it dived under. This croc was in the middle of the lagoon. In El Remate they told me that swimming where it's deep was the safest as the crocs like the shallows. Not this one!

VIEW FROM CHARLIES

15.05.21

I woke up to a beautiful sunrise, so I went to the beach to check it out when I noticed some movement at the turtle sanctuary. More turtles were born last night, and a volunteer, Ricardo, was going to free them. So, we did this together. In five minutes, all the baby turtles were safely at sea. How pretty and small and green, so dark it's almost black.

When I got back to my hut there was a lovely black female dog on my porch, and now, she is sleeping in my room! Today I'm also going to do a little bit of Spanish class with Ada, the primary school teacher of the island.

I had a good class with Ada, she is sweet, and we chatted for an hour, so I got to know things about her and about the island. I really enjoyed it and hope she won't get tired of doing this too soon. She wants nothing for it, and for now she is happy to do one hour a day. I am so lucky, how nice that someone I hardly knew, in five minutes decided to give me quite a lot of her time for nothing. And she's not a bad teacher at all! I'm clearing up some language doubts.

At the beach this afternoon, the most amazing scene: A hundred birds or more, Pelicans, small white birds that glimmered in the light, and this other birds, size of a seagull, crooked beak, long thin wings, all black with a white head (perhaps an albatross) were flying and circling and feeding for ages above the surfers' heads, and our heads, like a dance... They looked like ash abseiling and whirling in the wind after a massive fire. Very beautiful. Then I had a swim and some guy asked me if it was me who had been playing the harmonica. I was feeling really shy inside, obviously, but I was acting all normal about it. He plays too, it turned out, and may teach me a couple of blues tunes. It was quite surreal to have this kind of conversation. Who knows, maybe I am getting better...

16/05/21

Last night, another great storm, the sky noisy with thunder and lightning and heavy with rain. I was able to record it. For such a fine day as yesterday, today I woke up a bit moody, reflecting the colour of the sky and sea, so I went for a swim to clear my head, which helped. Then I walked on the beach up to, what I call, cactus point, where the sand gets flat and easier to walk on, where the waves at times sound like they are imploding, where there are hundreds of crabs of all sizes, colours and shapes. I noticed that they seem to know you are looking at them: whichever crab I was looking at, started to dart across the sand. I assessed this by just staring at different crabs without moving my body or head, just the eyes, and they seemed to respond to this by moving away if I was looking at them, then stopping as sion as I averted my gaze elsewhere... I also thought of the beach of Mazunte, almost crab free, and Goa in India, where there are many crabs. It looks to me like here there is less wildlife than in Asia in general. The crabs in India make many tiny balls of sand and create intricate, beautiful, random designs on the sand. I have seen similar designs only on the other side of the lagoon when I went with Amy and Bridget last week for lunch on the other side. On this beach the crabs dig one large hole.

VIEW FROM CHARLIES 2

17.05.21

Last night I bumped into Amy on the beach. Since it was her last night in Chacahua, we went for a drink on the rocks to watch the sunset and the skilled surfers riding huge waves. Then we went back to Telma's, the restaurant where Amy works, to prepare some margaritas to take to a small party at casa Tata, one of the hotels on the beach. Suddenly the restaurant got quite busy, so even I started to serve tables. After, we went to casa Tata, we played Domino, drank and ate

guacamole with other guests of the hotel. At one point two other guests returned and told us that a turtle was laying eggs just around the corner on the beach, so we all went to see this special moment. The turtle was big, and it was a magical moment. As it shuffled the sand back to cover the eggs, it made thumping sounds. Then it walked back to the sea. We were all high on nature then, and we returned to the hotel all excited and happy to have shared this moment together and had a few more drinks. Around 3 a.m. I walked back by the beach, my feet were leaving sparkling trails of blue in the water and also on the sand due to the bioluminescence, which was very beautiful. The sky was full of stars and pitch black like everything else, apart from the bioluminescence and the silvery crest of the waves. A truly magical night.

19.05.21

In Chacahua, they give out announcements to the town by blurting them over a PA system. I have started to understand what they say. Some announcements make me smile, like "Doña such and such has got tortillas and pig", or "Raymond, you have to go home ", or "Carlos, come back to the restaurant, someone wants to rent a surfboard". but mostly, we get a lot of "Raymond, your mum wants you home now!"

20.05.21

Everyone has gone, today I had that feeling that the beach was all mine, just like at Surf Camp at EL Paredon in Guatemala. The sea was calm and blue, and it was all about the pelicans. I love how they normally hang around the surfers in the waves. They are rather large and not particularly scared birds. Today I was able to swim pretty close to one, and have a good look. There were four of them bobbing in the water. I got really close to one and I was noticing how furry its head actually is, when I turned around, and there was another one behind me, watching me, even closer. Of course, when I turned around and saw it, it flew away. But it made me smile, because it felt like I had fallen for a distraction technique and they were actually studying me, not the other way around! I have been watching the ocean so much now. Today I noticed how the waves change speed, they speed up, slow down, the crest follows it, at times it surpasses it and crashes down, at times it lags behind.

I saw more turtle tracks last night, which I now recognise instantly. I followed them but the turtle had gone already. Later I had a beer with three Mexicans who are working on a beach hut, and were going through a crate of beer when I passed by, so they offered me one. Luis, Joseph, Artemio and I chatted a bit, the waves crashing inches from us, sitting under the starry sky. What a difference a half moon does, my walk was lit, unlike two nights ago when I came back from Casa Tata in pitch black. When I got home there was a big scorpion on my patio. I used a flip-flop to push him onto the sand below.

21.05.21

I just had a chat with one of the builders building the new hut beside mine. He told me they use a 4:4 mixture for the cement and stone.

Today I'm also waiting for Amy Maverick, a friend from London who came to Mexico just before the pandemic and decided to stay put.

22.05.21

Amy arrived yesterday with the last boat and we met up on the beach. So nice to see her after one year and a half, she was looking really well. We had a dinner and a nice catch up, then she went to bed as she was tired. I went for a walk on the beach.

This morning the sea is still calm! I'm going to have another very good beach day.

I don't know what it is, but I've been in a funny mood for the last couple of days, maybe because everyone left so suddenly. I have moments of exhilarating highs and suddenly I get quite restless or low, then, quite suddenly, I'm really happy again. This is my last week here, I think, I'll probably leave with Amy, so it will be easier to get a move on. Maybe this is also why I've been all over the place in the last few days: stirring in motion again, getting used to the idea of leaving, looking into the unknown, and looking at it from a place of Internet desolation. More power cuts on Chacahua mean it's impossible to load a map or look at a website. I hardly know where I am or where I'm going, so it's not easy to plan my next move without Internet.

I think I sparked a trend: now quite a few girls are wearing shorts on the beach rather than bikinis. I used to be the only one. Since yesterday there's two more, and another three in a hot pants cut rather than the whole revealing slip.

HARNAUD'S HUT

23.05.21

Well, Amy was looking really well, but yesterday morning she woke up feeling really ill in her stomach, so she spent all day in bed, hope she feels better today. I went for dinner alone, but was joined by Sandra, the lady that does the peyote ceremonies on the beach, and Romano, from Hungary, who's been living here for over 30 years. They just saw me there and decided to sit with me. Then also Louisa from Germany, who I met on the beach a few times, showed up at the restaurant and we asked her to join our table. We had a nice chat. Tuesday is going to be

Sandra's birthday and she will do a ceremony on the beach. I'll speak to Amy about it, we may go.

My landlord Carlos and family are not here today, so the kitchen is locked. I spent the morning jumping through the window a thousand times just to make a cup of coffee. Their kitchen has a window, and a large concrete outside sink attached to it. The window is actually a wooden frame with mosquito netting, which lifts up. Inside the kitchen, there is a little rope to which you can fasten this frame to keep the "hatch" open. So, I opened it from the outside and had to jump through to get my milk, cup and bowl, then boil the water for the coffee. I jumped back out carrying hot liquid to have my breakfast on my porch, washed up and then jumped again to put everything back. I guess I'll have to do this for the next three days because the whole family went with Carlos, and they won't be back till Tuesday!

24.05.21

No, I don't have to jump anymore! Harnaud, the French guy who lives in the hut opposite mine, told me where the keys to the kitchen are! Happy days.

The water has been great since the tide changed and the sea has swollen, eating away half the beach. Now during the day it's very calm and crystal clear, small clouds of sand puff up and explode in the last crest before the shoreline. The water has been so tempting that today, even the bloke with a cast on his arm (who had been freshening up on the shore with his arm up for the last few days) took it off and went in. Amy is also having a good time swimming. I am relieved because there's really not much else to do here, and especially since everyone is gone before she arrived, I was scared she was going to get too bored.

We decided to see the sunset from the lighthouse on the other side of the lagoon, so we boarded a lancha and then walked up the steep hill. By the lighthouse, there is another small outhouse, we climbed on its roof to watch the sunset. Luckily there was already a girl on top of the building who gave us a hand climbing up, her name was Emma, from France. From up here it is amazing. You can see the whole of Chacahua, surrounded by lagoon and ocean. You see the mainland stretching for miles, palm trees, cacti, smoke and mist in the distance, a few dirt roads, the lagoon snaking around with the lanchas drawing lines and silvery-pink ripples on the water as they travel along at sunset. A group of ten other guys and girls from USA, Mexico and France, joined us on the roof, they played music, and we chatted as the sun went down and the full moon rose. Then we all helped each other off the roof, which was nice. There was strong comradery: for some, going up or down was a bit scary or challenging.

Amy wanted to take some artistic pictures. She had some flammable material which makes lots of sparks when lit. We put this in a whisk attached to a string, then went to the little beach in the lagoon, so we could get water reflections. I lit up the material and swung it about above my head, whilst Amy took the pictures with a very slow shutter speed, and open iris, and we got some great pictures with circles of light with all this stuff coming off it, like a giant Catherine wheel.

Funny fact that happened when we were going to catch the boat. A guy came bursting out of his room on the first floor screaming, and completely naked just as we were passing below, so when he saw us, he just froze and closed the door again. We burst out laughing, and probably so did he, and whoever was with him in the room.

25.05.21

I went to practice the harmonica on the rocks and, by chance, found out how to play Karma Chameleon. I'm very happy with that.

26.05.21

These are the last few hours in Chacahua. Today I am leaving! Obviously, I don't really want to go, but Amy is going today, and I think that if I don't take advantage of this and go with her, I may never leave! Not exactly sure where I'm heading yet. I really enjoyed this magical island; I hope progress here it's not too fast. But who am I kidding? It's already changing fast.

The local people have been very nice, imagine that last night, a guy from the other side of the lagoon, who we met in a bar, even offered to share all his land with me, on the basis that I was a nice person. Everyone at Carlos cabañas made an effort to say goodbye. Arnaud told me he was listening to me playing on the beach the other night, but luckily, he didn't come to tell me at the time! He said "Maybe next time you come you could play some for us". Oh, how little does he know me!

27.05.21

Amy and I went to Puerto Escondido, and it's much nicer than I previously thought. Of course, it does help to go somewhere with friends. We went to a club on the beach and met up with Nuno and his girlfriend. Nuno left from the UK with Amy last year and he's also still here. He has a stall with clothes, jewellery and some tiny saxophones that he makes out of bamboo and pumpkin, they are awesome. I was only there for one hour because I had to board my night bus to Tuxtla.   I slept well on the bus, I woke up at dawn, the landscape was mountainous and full of deep green trees, the checkpoint went smoothly, although of course I got a bit scared. When we arrived, I had a few hours to kill, so I had a walk about this city, the capital of Chapas, had a chat with a man in the Main Square, watched some musicians play, and got a haircut. I was expecting this place to have an old centre, but again, it doesn't look like it. I only saw one very old building. I got back to the bus station for my second leg of the journey, three hours later I'm still here because the driver is late. This is going to be one hell of a journey. The first leg was twelve hours, then all this waiting, probably six hours now, and then the second bus ride will take more than twenty hours! This gets me to Tulum, which I'm not sure is my end destination either.

28/05/21

I woke up with jungle out of my window, arriving in Tulum around lunchtime. I wasn't quite sure what to do as the place is totally changed! I asked a guy for some info, and he said that renting on the beach was going to be very expensive and explained a few more things. So, I got a hostel really close to the coach station as it was quite clear from the start that I wouldn't stay here for very long. The hostel was really chilled, a haven of peace with a lovely courtyard. It's not on the beach but it's cool. I took a collectivo to the beach and met an Argentinian girl who told me where to get off to get on the beach. Man, there was actual traffic on the road behind the beach and you couldn't actually see the beach because the posh resorts have built walls and fences all along. They are marvellous structures made out of driftwood and other natural material with intricate designs and architecture, but wow! What a far cry from the simple place I remembered! There are boutiques, exclusive bars and hotels,

and, although all the buildings are quite tastefully hidden, they are still there and
something is lost. It didn't help that it is Sargasso seaweed season, so the normally pristine beach and the water didn't look at their best. I took a walk on the white beach and memories flooded back, how the white sand is cool underfoot even at 3 pm! When I found a section of the beach where I could not hear the music and chatter from the bars, it straight
away became that beautiful beach I remembered. The sound of the sea here is much mellower then on the Pacific. And yes, everything fell into place, and with no seaweed this is still a beautiful place, although I can't imagine seeing many iguanas here like I saw last time. What a shame, the change is immense. Around town there are also lots of Armed Forces and police at the moment as a drug war is going on, and people have been killing each other in the streets. I decided I will go away tomorrow to Mahaual, down the coast, as I hope that there will be no seaweed there. Beach access should also be a lot easier in this other town. In Tulum now, you can hardly get on the beach, because you have to go through the hotels or bars and some of them don't even allow you to just go through to the beach. Can you imagine? Just like Europe! What a shame. Don't get me wrong, this is also a very funky place, not completely commercial if you start looking around. But I'm not sticking around to find out. That's it, Tulum second time around, it's just an extremely quick visit. If there was no seaweed, I may have stayed a few days, but it's a mission to get to the beach, and there is definitely nowhere to practice the harmonica in peace, so you can see how, this time around Tulum is not for me.

29.05.21

Waiting at the station to go to Mahaual. The station is actually the only thing I recognise in the whole of Tulum. When I came here fifteen years ago it was a town with a population of 1000, now it's 25,000. It sat in the jungle, and you can still see bits of it, in the skilfully designed gardens of the bars on the beach, or on the few plots of land left in the town that have not yet been developed, where there are weeds and overgrown vegetation of tropical jungle type.

30.05.21

I arrive at Mahaual, find a room and hit the beach. They have sargasso here too, but they put some barriers up so the beaches are clear. This town is small and peaceful. A lot better than hyped, commercial Tulum. Suddenly I hear my name being called, it's Daniela, a childhood friend from Naples, I've known her since I was 15 years old! I had no idea she lives here now! I have not seen or heard from her for over three years! She is looking great, working in a diving centre. Obviously, we spend the rest of the day together, we go for sunset on the beach and a few of her friends join us, so that's great, I'm already meeting half the town! As we walk back to my hostel, we keep meeting people she knows, it takes ages to get home! It reminded me of life in El Remate where I would keep meeting people, and errands would take double the time as I stopped to chat with them.

We go for dinner at the corner bar where her friend Hugo is playing guitar and singing. He is very good, and the crowd loved it. Incidentally, Hugo and I live in the same hostel! How incredibly connected this whole adventure is becoming. Dani kindly offered me to stay with her, and I think I will, at least for a couple of days, whilst I understand how long I'll be here for. I'm very excited because Dani's friends are all divers, and they are the perfect people to take me snorkelling with turtles! Here the coral reef is so close, you can walk to it, but of course, you shouldn't, as walking on it would damage it, so you have to swim over it. I thought they were rocks in the distance, but Dani explained it is the actual reef, so I'm excited to go swimming a bit more and investigate. Because of the sargasso weed, and the season, the sea doesn't look particularly inviting (or definitely not what I was expecting) so it looks like that even here, I need a couple of days to adjust and shift my expectations! Just madness. Anyway, on my way here, I was wondering why I was actually going, why was I following a random suggestion made by someone I encountered randomly? It was German Louisa in Chacahua who told me to come here, and then, I come here and by "chance" I bump into Daniela. Or was it all part of a bigger design? The jungle really seems to have some different energy that makes things happen. You really feel it sometimes. Aside from hippy shit, at times the certainty of this is so strong, it's quite easy for me now to understand why for indigenous people these things are very real, why in the past people felt that things happen for a reason and believed, for example, that a flight of birds is a sign and could suggest what your next move should be. I wonder, what have we lost in Europe, in cities where we have no experience of these strong energies and no connection to Nature? Of course, it feels like a lot of crap to us, but actually, we are the ones that have no idea what these people are talking about. I think about my dad, his entire philosophy is based on reason and logic. He can't even begin to imagine that this other stuff might be true, that you can actually feel something.

The people of the town seem really nice. I've been to a few restaurants and shops and the locals are great. The town is also full of Italian expats, I could never live here! They are nice people of course, especially Roberto and Beatrice who make art with driftwood, really nice things. I told them, they are living my dream life. Maybe I'll go and talk to Roberto to see if I can help him in creating some of the pieces. Dani used to help him. I moved to her lovely house (weird to be in an actual house after all this time) and I really like the neighbourhood with its large Central Avenue and little square houses that look like little boxes. To me, it feels a bit like walking in some Californian suburb because the properties are bordered by green chicken wire mesh fences. I quite like the simple architecture of the houses which reminds me of the Moroccan houses of Tagazut. I'll probably stay with Dani a few days, she's been so nice, telling me I can stay the whole month if I want, but I may go to Holbox next week, as there is no Sargasso weed there. Daniela also has a tiny, tiny guitar. It's a bit hard to play but at least I'm doing it!

At sunset, we went to the lighthouse. Dani and her friends did Capoeira, whilst I found a faraway spot by the sea to play my harmonica.

31.05.21

I slept really well at Dani's. She's having a tooth pulled out later today, so I'm making a veg soup for the aftermath.

02.06.21

Dani didn't pull her tooth out yesterday as the dentist advised against it, until the infection clears out. So today we went snorkelling on the reef. There were loads of fish and plants, it was very magical and another world down there. But I didn't see any turtles.

04.06.21

For a second time we took the one-hour trip to the dentist by collectivo on the 60 miles long straight road to the crossroad where the town of Limone is situated, and this time the operation was a success. The tooth was out with not too much pain or hassle.

We also scored some pot from the pizza joint, bags are tiny here, compared to Chacahua! Less than half the amount!

07.06.21

We have been to a couple of parties in the last few days. A Leaving dinner for French-Canadian Elodie, where we spent the evening chatting, drinking and singing songs accompanied by an acoustic guitar. The other, a daytime housewarming party at Guatemalan metal artist Carlos and his family's new house. They were very happy with the new house and everyone was talking of what to plant in the spacious garden.

The best thing about this location seems to be the delightful breeze, which is almost constant, but it is sweet and mild and just perfect. Even when it's super-hot, the breeze really makes a pleasurable difference. I haven't been here in the Caribbeans long, but it seems to be the perfect climate, and the palm trees are the perfect trees to line the streets or dot the beach, drawing the ground with stripey shade, their heavy single leaves, dancing in the wind with the sound of shuffling flip-flops, stretch out well enough so you don't have to sit right under a coconut.

08.06.21

Dani and I went to the next town of Skalak, which was very small with all these wooden huts with cute pastel drawings on the side. I really liked it. There was almost no one. In the evening we went for an aperitif at Bea and Roberto's, the driftwood art people, and we cooked together some tempura. They have a really nice house full of their lovely artwork.

10.06.21

Although I was sad to leave Dani and Mahauhal, I decided I would go, so yesterday I travelled to Playa del Carmen, which is a really nice town, although quite big and busy. On the seafront they have a performance area where a show was going on, with people dressed in traditional clothes, capes made out of corn leaves, body paint, feathers. I had dinner watching a live band across the road, then went to my hostel and smoked outside for a while. I talked to a few people from the UK, Argentina, Peru and Tunisia. This morning I woke up early and after breakfast I actually achieved something amazing: I walked in the music shop and bought a small guitar before going to catch the coach and ferry to Holbox. Well, I can't believe I did it!

On the coach I met Joseph and since he booked in the same place I have booked, we decided to share a ride there. There are no roads or cars on the island of Holbox, the taxis are golf carts. It's a lot more built-up than Chacahua with even a few three-story buildings, quite a few bars and restaurants, some shops selling gifts or clothes, a couple of barber shops, and even a paved square! I am staying in a tent at a campsite by the beach, it is a very peaceful place.

13.06.21

A-G

I am totally out of reach.

I have a tent on the beach.

I swim with the pelicans and the dogs,

And at night I hear the frogs.

I am in Holbox in the rain

I am in Holbox in the rain.

There are mosquitoes everywhere

you would think that I should care

But I step in puddles all day long,

and I think about a song.

Let's have a strum around the fire,

count shooting stars till we tire.

Because here the time stands still,

so, you get more time to feel.

I am loving Holbox. The other morning, I went swimming and was joined by a very clever and cute dog. He was totally black against impossibly white sand and the turquoise sea. He wanted to sit on my lap, so we just stayed there, lolloping in the water.

It's rainy season and the sandy roads become rivers, so it's easier not to ever wear shoes here. The sand is white and never gets hot, so it's fine to walk barefoot all day. The other night, there was live music in town, and everyone ended up dancing barefoot in the muddy streets dodging the golf carts, sitting on the pavement outside the club. I had a great time and met a few people, including four buskers from Puebla who play drums and Djembes.

The Campsite I am staying at had been suggested to me by Claudia from Portugal, who I met at El Paredon in Guatemala, it's a very special place close to the beach. Everyone is laid back and I am even able to play the guitar in my tent, when it rains, and I know no one else is around. At times I go and play the harmonica on the beach. We are surrounded by mangroves here, and the mosquitoes are hell. The first couple of days it was really hard, then I invested in all sorts of repellents and spirals and it got a lot better. You have to spray yourself before you leave your tent and continue to apply the repellent throughout the day. If you go to the toilet at night, you better remember to spray yourself! And light up mosquito coils in the areas in which you intend to hang out, even in the daytime.

I went to explore one side of the island, almost up to Punta mosquito, where you can't walk anymore as it is a bird sanctuary. I saw two pink flamingos flying towards the sunset. Here white sand banks form at low tide, and the water, at dusk reflects colours impossible to describe. Up to this point, there are nice bars and restaurants on the beach, but crucially, compared to Mahaual, the beach is very wide and the bars don't take up all the space and don't have tables going all the

way to the water edge so there is plenty of room for people to lie on the beach on towels.

15.06.21

When it rains, it really pours. Some bits of the road and areas the campsite are becoming hard to negotiate. Hopefully not to the point of having to leave. Needless to say, the mosquitoes are loving this.

CANDY'S CARPA

16.06.21

BALAM CAMPSITE

17.06.21

COCINA

It has been raining non-stop all night and all day, hopefully it'll stop by 6:00 p.m. Lio and Vicky, the two managers of the campsite, made a bridge with planks so we can access the bathrooms and showers without getting totally wet as the access to them is completely flooded. This way I can also go to my tent without wading through the puddle which is now almost knee-high. It also scares me a bit going through it at night as there is a chance now that a croc would be here. With all the water we had, our puddles have joined to the lagoon where the croc lives.

At least, all this rain has given me the chance to draw and hang out with everyone at the campsite. At one point there was quite a few of us, including Candy the dog. Now only Joseph and I are left here with the staff, hoping not to be washed away. This morning Mattias, one of the volunteers working here, made us taste Mate (an herbal infusion) and talked about the ceremony of it, which was interesting. It's very popular in Argentina and other South American countries, and it's drunk in a cute cup with a metal straw. The drink is shared amongst everyone, drinking from the same straw (even during Covid times!). It was very refreshing.

20.06.21

The rain finally stopped, and for two days, it was all about the flamingos. Rows of eight or nine flying through the sky, their long necks bending a little, shiny pink in the light blue of the sky, what a spectacle. It was all about animals in general. Everyone came out after the rain, all kinds of fish, including the stingrays, insects, birds and even the crocodiles. Two nights ago, the lagoon and the flooded roads were connected to each other. On our way to a gig, we saw a crocodile really close to the campsite. We were scared but luckily since then the water has receded a bit, so it's unlikely that the croc' is still about.

Because of the muddy puddles, one of the cuts on my leg got infected and became green, so today I had to scrape it off by hand. It didn't hurt, hope I did enough and now I am trying to avoid puddles. The sea has been gorgeous, blue, turquoise and white, I'm just so happy here at the campsite with people coming and going, speaking Spanish and generally hanging out. Last night we made a lovely fire under the stars.

I have also discovered that if you put the spirals on the beach during the day, no insect comes to bother you, including horseflies, and you can actually chill out on the beach!

22.06.21

The puddles have almost dried out in the campsite and in the streets. Even the knee-high one at the crossing, but more rain is forecast for the next four days. Hopefully it won't be as bad as last week…in any case, later I'm heading out into town to buy groceries, as there is a chance that I'll get stuck here for days. In the meantime, I enjoy the beach, the sea has been marvellous.

Yesterday, I went to watch the sunset at the beach, and for the first time I took the guitar out! That was a big step, but I really enjoyed it and I didn't mind too much if people walked past. At one point three people approached, so I stopped playing and offered them the guitar. One of them picked it up and started playing it in the shallow water. If anyone passed by, he'd ask what song they wanted to hear, and it was really funny to see the various reactions, the songs that people asked for. We watched the sunset together, then we all went our separate ways. Since yesterday, I am the only guest at the campsite, as all the other guests have not been able to handle the mosquitoes, and left before giving themselves the chance to get used to it. I'm loving it here. Gabby, Matty, Lio and Vicky, who volunteer here are really nice and we get on great.

The 31st of July, date when this trip ends, is approaching fast and for the last few days, every now and then, this thought has kept popping into my head, filling me with dread. I am certainly still not ready to go home. I try to push these thoughts away as soon as they surface.

24.06.21

Three people so far on this trip have asked me if I'm ill. They all have come out with it out of the blue, very abruptly and directly. I feel fine, I hope they're not like those dogs smelling cancer, alerting me of an illness I don't even know I have.

The campsite filled up again; musicians, dancers and families are passing by this time, and we are sharing nice nights by the fire in the full moon, singing songs and playing guitar.

Gabby told me to put my sandals back on to avoid being eaten alive by the ants. What a weird feeling to be wearing shoes after two weeks walking barefoot, they felt very spongy and soft! but I much prefer walking barefoot.

25.06.21

Europe is certainly getting closer; the bags of weed are getting a lot smaller.

Last night we all hung out at the campsite and watched the supermoon together. I made a kind of guacamole for my dinner, and everyone had some, including Mexican people. I am slowly improving on my "hide the potatoes" syndrome, by which I mean I don't like to cook for other people because I am afraid they won't like it. I have shared something I have cooked a few times now, my unease with it is getting slightly better.

People have also been telling me that my Spanish is very good, which is very nice of them but it's not true. It's fair to say I am improving though.

26.06.21

I've taken to hang out by the fire pit in the morning and I amuse myself watching the iguanas sunbathing, fighting, chasing each other or become enlarged and stand in that domineering stunt, tilting their head up and down.

FOGATA BALAM

29.06.21

The other night Alan, a young Mexican with a lovely temperament and an infectious loud laugh that resonates throughout the campsite, showed me how to make "adobo", a Mexican sauce with different chilies. It was lovely! And interesting to find out how it was done.

Yesterday, I went to Punta mosquito which is a sandbank in the middle of the sea, close to the lagoon and the mangrove, a reserve for flamingos and other birds. I had to cross the water, which was knee high, stepping in muddy sand close to the mangrove. What an adrenaline rush, a five-minute crossing holding my bag containing my phone over the top of my head so it wouldn't get wet, with fear of getting stuck in the quicksand first, then step on a stingray or meet a crocodile. But, when I got there, two flamingos with their long necks were quite close, heads in the water, eating. Behind them, amongst other birds, there were six more in a line. I stayed there to admire them for a while, pink against the light blue sea and white sand. Then I headed back as I didn't know for how long the tide would stay low.

The girls asked me to volunteer here at the campsite, by tomorrow I have to accept or decline.

YOGA SPACE

1.07.21

Yesterday, I did my first shift at the campsite, I'm doing a trial week. Duties include, cleaning kitchen, bathrooms and showers, getting rid of trash, preparing the tents with air mattresses, and hopefully matching sheets, but the best thing of all, partly why I accepted the job, is looking after the garden. I don't need this job, but I'm happy to help the guys to run this place for a while and to busy myself doing something. I have to admit, it was a bit of a shock, actual work, after so long! I haven't actually done this kind of job for over 20 years. There may be better things I could be doing, but this work takes only four hours in the morning, so there's still plenty of time for anything else. The hardest and most important job of the shift though, is to prepare the rich vegan breakfast for the staff. It includes iced fresh pineapple and orange juice, vegan oat pancakes with banana slices and peanut butter, some freshly made mini breads, which we make in the pan as we have no oven here, guacamole (they loved mine) and lentil or chickpea houmous (depending on what we have). They are masters at this, I took ages to do it and needed Vicky's help, but they tell me that it's normal at the beginning. I am super happy to be learning this breakfast, it's something I will definitely do when I want a pancake (of which I've become quite addicted on this trip). Another good thing about working is that I'm smoking a bit less!

04.07.21

There has been the most beautiful sky for the past few nights, and I have seen some shooting stars. The sunsets have been amazing too. The other day, as I was walking to Punta mosquito, just before sunset, I noticed the weirdest optic effect in the sand which happened on a couple of occasions. The footprints and shapes in the dazzling white sand looked like they were bulging out, rather than being deep impressions in the ground. I've never seen it before, it was like looking at a computer-generated image.

I have been in two minds about the job, as these are my last few weeks here. Why do this, and not something else? I suppose it's laziness. If anything, I realise that I'm not ready to go home, there are so many more places I'd like to visit, there is another place close by that I'd like to go to, as I've heard good things about it, but I feel there is not enough time. I will decide at the end of this week's work, to either stay, or leave this island. Holbox is cool, laid back and beautiful, but it is no paradise, lately there is constant noise and buildings are going up faster and faster. Holbox is already dead as far as a natural paradise is concerned, the sad thing is that no one seems to notice, they think we're still just heading there.

05.07.21

SOMOS INSTANTES

They've stopped making a noise for now! At least at the beach right outside the campsite, which is just perfect. Here, when they're not building, it is incredibly peaceful as we are far away from town, and this is almost our private beach!

Today, the sea was "rough", there were "waves", which means mini waves one centimetre high. They formed on the usually pond-like water, giving out a playful, joyous vibe. I saw a dolphin very close to the shore at sunset. It was feeding and spent a long-time swimming very close. Back at camp, I saw a shooting star.

06.07.21

Today, I made breakfast. I needed some help from Vicky, getting everything ready, but I smashed it with the little breads, which had lots of air inside, and the hotcakes which were thin, round, and consistent.

I found a new perfect spot on the beach, under a palm tree, I don't think many people come here. Hopefully I can make it mine.

Funny how things that happen miles away in Europe can still upset me or annoy me, and bring me right back to it, even if I'm sitting on a beautiful beach, staring at the gorgeous sea.

Tomorrow, I'll have to decide whether to keep volunteering. I am still in two minds about it, partly because I am not helping a local business, the owners are French and Argentinian. Usually, I am totally against volunteering in this fashion, but I like the girls and they asked me, so I would not mind hanging out with them, and live this lifestyle for a while. A simple job right by the beach, with loads of free time to do my own thing.

07.07.21

On my little beach I saw a snake, and black dragonflies came to rest on my sari whilst I was playing guitar. Last night, I tried to play the harmonica, it was full of sand, it almost choked me. More notes have stopped working, it's had it now. I miss playing it, although I have abandoned it a bit, partly because it really is too loud against the Caribbean Sea. This is not the roaring Pacific.

When it got dark, but before the moon rose, I went to see the bioluminescence in the lagoon at Punta Coco, with a French couple and a Spanish guy who arrived at the campsite. When shaking and moving the water, the bioluminescence made green luminescent trails, it was everywhere, beautiful. On the way back, we walked by the beach to see more stars. Here we encountered a group accompanied by a guide who was showing them the constellations by pointing a laser at the sky. It's a very cool and extremely effective way to show the sky. You can really see what he's pointing at.

10.07.21

On my little beach I saw two very cute bunnies. It is amazing the number of different animals that pass by this spot. The island at the moment is full of Europeans: British, Germans, and Italians have arrived.

12.07.21

The other night, an Austrian guy who was staying at the campsite got stung twice by a scorpion on the beach. Luckily for him, the poison of the scorpion on this island doesn't actually kill you. His leg, face, and tongue got paralysed for a while, and he wasn't a hundred percent for a couple of days.

This morning, I got up early, went to do yoga on the beach and six flamingos flew very close, squiggly necks, long legs, frantically beating the smallish wings, all pink, with a black stripe on one side of the wing. What a precious moment for me alone.

15.07.21

Last night, we made pizzas for Alan's birthday, in the pan, as we have no oven, delicious.

17.07.21

Two weeks to go until my flight, and I am starting to really panic. Why am I going back exactly? I have to think of it as part of the journey, a few months in Europe. But I don't really want to go back to a normal house, sleeping in the bed, spend all day inside, watching the news and the TV, taking the trains, going to work. I'd be ready to leave Holbox, but only to do some more travelling, to explore more of Mexico, not to go home. Holbox is not really Mexico. Actually, it doesn't feel like I've seen much of the real Mexico at all, having mainly been to small seaside, touristic locations. Here, at Balam, I've learnt a lot about Argentinians. They're almost more Italian than the Italians, it makes me laugh and I tell them all the time. They love cooking from scratch, and they are indeed great chefs. The Argentinian also seem to love Quintana Roo, they pretty much own Holbox and Playa del Carmen. The little Mexican culture I'm encountering, is brought by the few Mexicans that choose to stay here at Balam. Only Alan has become a semi-permanent fixture here, with his good vibes and loud laugh, and he's teaching me loads about Mexico and its customs.

The camp has been full all week and I've loved all the different vibes created by those that visited. At the moment, there is a French family with four children, two Colombians, a mother and daughter who look like sisters, Frederick from France who reminds me of my childhood friend Fabrizio, Chris from Bournemouth, obviously Alan, a few more people, and this morning, finally Lio, has left to go to the US to chop weed, which is something that everyone seems to be doing to get quick cash, if they manage to get into the country.

18.07.21

Last night must have been a special one. This morning I saw three sets of turtle tracks, they came to nest. I went for a lovely swim, and as I was drying on the beach, I saw two dolphins.

I have been thinking about what to do, and I realise now, that it all boils down to; do I want to travel and have small jobs as and when needed? Or do I want to build a career? This month has shown me that I could totally live like this for the next 30 years or so.

21.07.21

I went for an early walk yesterday morning; as I got to the beach, I had the feeling I was going to see many animals, and yes, I saw three dolphins. Sometimes I just know it's going to happen! Nature rewards you sometimes: it's happened twice already, for example, that whenever I think I should leave the beach to find an internet connection or else, but instead I choose to linger, I get to see the dolphins.

Alan and I went to Punta Ziricote to catch the sunset, we saw a flamingo flying low, so close to us we could see every detail, even the feathers, and the different shades. Another flamingo landed on the sandbank, and we were able to watch it for a while, until some tourists got too close and it flew away, only to return once more and giving us a great show flying all around the lagoon, black against the sunset, then pink over the lagoon as it circled a few times to gain altitude, and then flew away into the distance. This was a proper show, and we were able to admire it for quite some time, mega-special.

22.07.21

Last night, we all went to see Matty playing at Tribu bar, and then went to dance in the street outside the Hot Corner, because it was Alan's last night and he loves the Hot corner. Incredibly, today, after one month, Alan left! We're going to miss his positive attitude and infectious laugh. There are almost no guests at the camp after two very busy weeks, and a succession of hasty departures due to either too many mosquitoes and biting ants, or heat in the tent or lack of Internet.

23.07.21

It's so nice to do a bit of gardening at the camp and notice the different simple things that go on. Even raking, every day it's a different kind of thing that's fallen down, today some flowers, yesterday leaves, tomorrow a little pear-shaped fruit that the iguanas love to eat. It's also very pleasing to do weeding in a garden with no soil, just sand, as it's not hard work. We rake everything off. We don't leave a layer of mulch. I'd like to have mulch, as I think it also helps with bordering areas, creating paths and adding colour, but the trend here is to rake it all away, so be it. Once I got used to it, I have to agree, either the mulching is purposely and neatly done, or all leaves must go. It's an "all or nothing "situation.

25.07.21

This morning I went to Punta Coco, and I saw a flamingo really close and flying very low. I saw him coming so I was ready to really take a good look at it when it flew overhead.

I haven't spent any time mentioning the sunsets and the cloud formation here in Holbox. They are immense. The clouds remind me of Japanese cloud drawings or mountains or explosions. Every sunset is a dramatic, incredible moving painting in pink, purple, blood orange and gold. You have to see it to believe it.

Today was my last day volunteering at the campsite, as it's my last week here in Holbox. I have been barefoot for three months, hardly have been in enclosed spaces for the last six and have been camping for the last two. I am not ready to go back to the city. I have one million thoughts and yet I'm paralysed. Why do I choose to do what I believe is expected of me and not what I really want to do? People ask me why I am going back, and I don't have an answer.

26.07.21

How easy it is to catch a fish for experienced birds, but how hard it is to keep that catch and eat it in mid-air, as the slippery pray sometimes wriggles free and plunges impossible heights back to the safety of the water, or other birds come to try and snatch it.

The sound design of the island has dramatically improved as most work around us seem to have temporarily stopped. The boys with the big machines went to Merida for a few days and we get to hear the nature again. I haven't bothered trying to record any but, one difference I've noticed in the sound of the water, is that here, since the beaches are made of shells, you can totally hear a "shelly" quality as the water laps through them. It sounds a bit like the beach in Brighton, although that's a pebble beach and therefore the sound is definitely "stonier".

The absence of building work actually makes me think about it, so this morning I have been thinking of the fact that the sound of construction, once begun, will never stop, till the end of time. It's a bit like the funeral pyres on the Ganges River at Varanasi, which were lit in a very distant time never to be extinguished again, as there is always a body to be cremated and there always will be, till the end.

This morning I went to Punta Coco as I knew I'd catch a flamingo (our meetings just before 8 AM are becoming a thing) and sure enough, as soon as I got there, one swooped down, super close to the shore where I was standing and super low, it circled a couple of times and went to land in the middle of the lagoon. There it waded through the water and stood on one leg, the other one bent at two impossible angles, and it let me admire it undisturbed for over half an hour, the lagoon all to ourselves. A special moment.

The lagoon at Punta Coco, but especially at Punta Ziricote, reminds me a lot of El Remate. There is a wooden pier, the water is often still like a lake, and in the distance, you see the Mexican coast, low, flat and green, almost reflecting on the water and dissolving in the distance like a painting, a lot like the view from Mon Amy, only further away and bigger.

30/07/21

I haven't done a lot of writing this week, as I've done a lot of thinking. And nothing, in the end I decided to try and stay here till April!!! (Or earlier if the money runs out, but I'm going to try). There is still Covid in Europe and working or socialising will be hard. I don't have much to go back to so quickly, and I just hope work will still be there when I go back! Now I'm ready to go and explore Mexico, go back to Guatemala or Columbia to renew my Visa and to do some proper volunteering in the jungle or similar. I am so glad I've actually come to this conclusion, and I've made my mind up.

The sea has been wonderful in the last few days, the island's way of talking to me, and this morning, when I went to Punta Coco to think for the last time if I should go or stay, my flamingo friend was already waiting for me, this time really near, he was feeding on the seashore. With the long legs, a flamingo pats the floor with a funny kind of dance and scoops out the food from the sand. I sat on the beach at a respectful distance, and he didn't fly away, so we were able to share at least half an hour in each other's company, with no one else, apart from other birds. In the end I left before him, but my mind was made up by now, thanks to him, nature, the lovely people of the campsite and me, finally really listening to my heart, and really being spontaneous. Sunday I will leave here to continue my adventure. I am so ready!

03.08.21

Well, I am still in Holbox! I suddenly got offered a dream paid job as in-house live sound engineer at a hostel on the island where they have live music six nights a week, and I took it, as I thought it may be fun to do something like this for a while (till the hurricanes come) meet people and socialise without having to necessarily drink. This is how I know I took the right decision to stay. When you follow your heart and do something right, you get unexpected gifts, especially on this island. Real Mexico will have to wait a little longer.

12.08.21

It's the first time I write since I started working. I was getting worried that working had sucked any creative juice out of me as for the last 10 days I have done no writing, drawing or playing guitar. Then, since yesterday, I seem to have started it all again, thankfully. Probably I was just tired and getting used to the new routine. It was all a bit of a shock, it's the first time in ages that I have a regular job with a boss, I have been self-employed, and my own boss for years. At work everyone is nice and have welcomed me. We've had a week of live music, jazz, DJ live set with live musicians, a band, a salsa night, jam night, and an open mic night. I got to learn the room and now it's all sounding okay. I also had to troubleshoot and fix things. It's funny to be the only one in charge of the whole place. I had never done that before. It's also been a very long time since I last "worked" in music, so I have many contrasting feelings, and flooding memories. I am having lots of fun though, it's great, especially now that I feel comfortable with the whole system.

Funny how, as I address musicians during sound check, often I automatically switch to English almost without noticing. Like, it just feels so natural to have this kind of conversation in English. Of course, it's only a few words, then I catch myself doing it and switch back to Spanish where possible. Although I don't always like the music, this is a great experience. Living right on a beautiful beach, go and soundcheck at 5 pm, then have time to watch the always magical sunsets, then go back to work listening to some music for a few hours in a very popular hostel with loads of people having a good time. A dream lifestyle worth trying! Yesterday I got quite an elated feeling and, although Holbox is a bit of a resort, I was happy to finally be one of the locals and thought, "yes, I can give this thing a try." There are moments, when it's quiet, that this place is pure paradise.

The sunsets in Holbox are great, because of the colours and the layers of different cloud types that draw shapes in the sky. But regardless of the clouds, it seems to me that the sun never fails to hit the sea, you always get to see at least a bit of it touching down. And the sun here looks huge. Sometimes it's tinted shades of violet or blood orange, Scarlett, and pink. The mornings too, sometimes have a flamingo pink hue, with the silvery sea dappling below, and on days like these, you just know it's going to be a flamingo day and you are going to see one.

17.08.21

Yesterday was a day of butterflies and dragonflies. The sky was full of colourful flutter. It was very hot and sticky, and now we are bracing ourselves for our first hurricane. Apparently, we're right in the middle of its path, and it's coming tomorrow. None of us has ever been in one and we're not sure what to do or whether it's safe to be here. I had heard it was coming a few days ago and chose not to say anything about it to Vicky, because I knew she would be scared, in the hope that the hurricane would eventually not come here. But, as it's now clear we're going to get it, yesterday we were all talking about it, and she told me she also hadn't mentioned anything to me for the same reason that I am very scared of heavy winds, and she didn't want to worry me unduly.

On a happier note, finally I saw mapaches! As I left work, a family of raccoons was scavenging in the street and drinking water from the street that's now turned into a river of mud. Mama raccoon with four cute fluffy little kits. As I walked home on the beach, a bright halfmoon was lighting the sky so that I didn't need to switch on the torch on my phone to see where I was going. A Silvery twinkle on the oily black water and a brightness I had forgotten, since the last few days of the new moon and meteor showers had been intensely dark. The other night, me Vicky and Canadian-Taiwanese Andy, one of the new arrivals, went to lie on the beach to see the shooting stars, but I didn't see too many.

I have been considering that walking barefoot not only connects me to the Earth in a different way, keeping me aware and in the moment, it also teaches me and reminds me of my fragility and, ultimately, mortality. Walking barefoot is meditating, as you end up taking every step consciously, really taking in what's here and now, because as soon as you don't do that, you usually end up kicking something or step on something sharp, and you know that that's not a great idea, one wrong step and this trip could be over, just like that.

23.08.21

The hurricane came and went with little damage to the campsite. As a precaution, we had closed it, took up all the tents and put all the kitchen items and other stuff in a cabaña and went to stay in town. I stayed where I work, but the hurricane was not stronger than a British storm. The main water pipe to the island has been damaged though, and the whole island has been without water for the last three days. At work it's been hard with so many people there, and only water delivered in buckets. There was a small revolt from the staff, concerned about using valuable water just to keep the bar open, whilst others are rationing their drinking water, but in the end, they decided they will stay open.

Yesterday there was a festival at work, we talked about the environment and the effects of pollution on the island. It was great for me because I'm finally getting to know some locals and they are people with some social conscience. I might get involved in some growing project or a cleaning project.

Yesterday I also had a chat with Gino, one of the owners of the campsite. He had been told by Vicky that I turned down the offer of a free apartment from work, to stay at the campsite, so he offered me to stay here on my own for free when the campsite closes in mid-September for the worst of the hurricane season. This is a fantastic development. Actually, having this place all to myself would be amazing, I was actually dreading having to organise a different accommodation.

03.09.21

I love to lie down under a palm tree on the beach and look at the blue sky through it. I've been doing loads of that. I've also noticed that the shade the trees make is larger now, perhaps a combination of the plants obviously growing over time, but also the position of the earth in relation to the sun due to the changing of the season.

Last night at work we had open mic, which is always great fun, and last night, I thought it all sounded particularly good! I am also getting to know more people outside the campsite, which is nice.

07.09.21

The last few nights have been pitch dark as I've been coming back late, the sea black, the sand black and the crane wading in the shallows, stark white. There was a huge storm last night too, and I watched it from the comfort of the patio at the hostel, smoking a joint, watching the fat drops coming down on the plants and shimmering through the garden lightbulbs and street lights. Then there was a short power cut. But Holbox seems to love me, it never rains when I have to go out or return home.

After the rain, the sea is always amazing, and today I saw a huge stingray swimming in front of me, what a moment.

08.09.21

08.09.12 -BALAM

I made my first vegan carrot cake in the pan yesterday. It was delicious, apart from the fact that it was salty, not sweet, as I put too much baking soda. Luckily it was a carrot cake, therefore it was acceptable for it to be savoury (my nan actually used to have a savoury carrot cake recipe). But we were all left with a desire for sweetness, so Anna, the new volunteer, made a lovely apple cake.

Gabby and I went to Punta Ziricote. It has been a long time since I last went there, and it looked absolutely gorgeous. It was Gabby's first visit and she loved it too. We saw a few stingrays, and a very big one too. My second in as many days. Different migratory birds are now visiting, (I have no idea what they are!)

The girls are leaving Holbox in a week and the campsite is falling apart around us. Maybe I won't be able to stay here after all. Hopefully they'll fix it.

It's a week of rain, Rizla gets stuck together. Here I've learnt that you can lick the glue strip and it's much easier to peel them back apart.

The other day, I also lost my wallet.

14.09.21

The moon set early in the last few days and, coming back home at night the other day there was an incredible amount of bioluminescence. It was visible as the waves broke on the shore, a thin line of blue light running along the sand, beautiful. Loads of dots of light in the sand, and I could see light around the fish, swimming in the water, I saw a fish flying, all shimmer and light. What a show.

I had to sleep at the hostel for a couple of nights this week because around the campsite it is pretty flooded right now, and I was a bit scared of crocodiles coming back in pitch black at night. The puddle still goes half way up my leg, but I've conquered the fear and for the last two days I've been coming back.

15.09.21

Often the animals (especially insects) dictate how you live your day, and if you try and fight it, you're not going to have a good time. You have to flow, you have to know the island, you have to know the habits of the animals and know where to go and at what time. Many people leave the campsite because it's all too much, too overwhelming when you first get here, after the rain, when the mosquitoes are at their worst and they don't know how to escape them. Go with the flow and most times you are rewarded. Today for example, I left early in the morning and the sea was just amazing. I went to sit on the pillow-shaped white rocks that come out into the water like halfmoons, and there were a lot of cute fish I've never seen before.

It's the last day of the campsite. The girls are putting everything away and in a couple of days I'll be here alone.

18.09.21

The girls left yesterday, but I'm not exactly alone yet, for Lio, who came back from trimming weed in the USA, decided to stay one more week. And there is Comi the cat of course, heavily pregnant, so I guess soon it will be me and an undisclosed number of cats. The water pump stopped working so we are using buckets to wash, the old faithful. When I had my first bucket shower yesterday, as the water hit me, memories of Indian bathrooms started flooding back. I embraced it straight away!

I am loving having the campsite all to myself in the morning, and today I have managed to do a bit of yoga. I can finally see myself keeping up with this routine. I felt way better afterwards for doing it and I have smoked less first thing in the morning, so I am pretty pleased. And of course, I'm loving being able to play the guitar in the "lounge" area of the campsite, without having to hide somewhere in the tent or on the beach.

These have been days of pelicans. I even saw one catching fish, his beak engorged and moving with the flapping prey. The midges on the beach have been awfully annoying lately. The moon is almost full again and I am once again at the midpoint of this trip, therefore it's already the beginning of the end, I can't believe it! Although it's still six and a half months away.

19.09.21

Last night, David, one of the volunteers at the hostel, organised a party on the beach for his best mate Alex's birthday. I helped him source the speaker for the surprise party with Bove, Alex's favourite DJ of the island. She is probably my favourite too, that I've heard play when I work. She's from Uruguay and plays some tribal funky tunes.

Everything was perfect, the moon, almost full, the cobalt black sea, the beach, the people, the drink. I was just thinking how happy I was to be there, the first proper party of the trip, and indeed from before Covid. And then the police came and shut us down after only a few minutes, and they came with armed Navy officers. Anyway, everyone else was already on drugs, so they were desperate to find another location for this party. I went home at this point as I had shopping on me and didn't fancy, not being on drugs, waiting for the party to kick off again somewhere else. I was very sad to leave. But it was already 3:30 AM when I got home anyway. I sound very old, I know, but I promised myself to never again shop for fresh veg in the evening, so that I won't miss any more parties. On my walk home, for the first time, I saw raccoons in the shallow sea! Who would've thought.

20.09.21

Yesterday evening, after soundcheck, something incredible happened. I picked up a guitar, and jammed for a few minutes with Gina, who works at the hostel's reception but also makes music, and Cesar, our in-house percussionist. Gina had begun playing the drums when I decided to play along, then Cesar, who was still hanging around after soundcheck, started to sing. Davide, who owns the place, suddenly came upstairs. This stopped me from playing, so he asked me why I had stopped and said he had come up because of the music and wanted to see who was playing. The owner of the guitar later told me he liked what he heard. Do I believe them?

At the end of the jam session that night, Davide also complimented me on the engineering as he's done it too, and he knows how hard it is to get a sound especially during the live jam, with many people playing, singing, switching mics, instruments and having different ranges, volumes and abilities.

24.09.21

I have never mentioned the seaweed, as I thought it was one detail too many, but now I have to because of something that I witnessed yesterday. There are balls of seaweed that roll on the seabed like tumbleweed in the wind. You look through the crystal-clear water, and it's like looking at a submerged desert, with tumbleweeds here and there. Yesterday I saw a shoal of small fish, possibly sardines. They moved so coolly as one in the water and they formed balls which looked like tumbleweeds, even mimicking the way they move in the water. What a way to disguise yourself and confuse predators, I guess that's why they do it. I followed them for a while, watching, when a girl passed by us in the opposite direction. When she got close the fish started to go in a circle in unison, swirling until she had passed us completely, then they moved off again like one brain.

25.09.21

I am getting to know people better and it's starting to feel really good. Last night I joined the bar staff after work, and we went to Mahi where they were playing some techno! (Yeah) so we bopped around for a while, until they closed for the night. It was nice.

27.09.21

I'm left on my own at the campsite. Lio, and his dad who had come to visit for a week, left today. Who knows if and when I will see Lio, Vicky and Gabby again.

It's Monday. I went to the beach, practically empty. It really feels like I have the island all to myself. It's the last week of work, and soon we'll all leave. Holbox right now is truly a paradise. Nice to have the campsite all to myself to play guitar anywhere any time I like. I think I'm going to enjoy this week.

29.09.21

Even most of the mosquitoes seem to have left. Result! So nice to hang out here at Balam, listen to the birds, watch the purple dragon flies that are around lately, cook some nice meals, do some yoga, have a chilled beer.Last night I played guitar by the fire, mind you, there was no roaring fire or people... but still, I played in the circle, under the stars, and what a starry night it was. It was Tuesday, my day off, so I got to enjoy the campsite in the evening.

I got a cold, not covid I think, but I am keeping people at arm's length and didn't swim.

01.10.21

I had a great time at the open mic. Most of the people that performed put on a good show. The musician who came to host the gig, Selinda Cordoba was really bluesy and sang and played guitar very well. Her original songs were also funny; I really enjoyed her music. The night was made the more exciting as Rami, keyboard player of Foo Fighters, came to play! He's a very nice, mellow guy and he could obviously play really well. The place rocked big time and it sounded good too. A very welcomed change from the usually more Latin feel of the gig. Rami told me it was the first time he could hear himself well when playing there, which obviously made me very happy.

02.10.21

RECEPCIÓN

Today, I finally managed to get a ticket to Colombia after 3 days of trying, Result! Very exciting, I can now get back into gear and focus on how to get off this damn island. Of course, I also don't want to leave, it's so deserted now, it's just amazing... but I really need to do a Visa run.

03.10.21

What a momentous day, I'm leaving Balam camping after over three months, I can't even believe it. I've packed up my tent and put all the kitchen stuff away in the cabaña, almost in automation. It's not quite sinking in yet that when I walk out of that gate later today, with my small rucksack, it's going to be for the last time. I've loved it here, what a place, shame for all the construction work going on around me. I am glad I've seen it now, before it's too late, as, I guess, once the hotels are built, this side of the island won't be the same again. Already, yesterday, at the beach just by the campsite, there were two new notices of no trespassing. One was attached right on the palm tree we usually shade under.... so sad.

I'm going to spend the next two nights at the hostel before leaving the island, tonight is the last night before they shut for refurbishments and the worst of the rainy season, so we are going to have a blast. I'm planning to go to El Cuyo on Tuesday (finally!) and then, off to Colombia for 6 weeks, before returning here to do the Xmas season at the hostel... or at least that's the plan... I am going to leave some of my things here, at Lorena's, my manager. I hope I won't regret it.

07.10.21

I've finally managed to leave Holbox and go to El Cuyo! The last few days in Holbox have been really nice, I hung out with the people at the hostel. We had a very good week of music, closed by a brass band from Tulum who were great and were very nice guys.

Anita, who works behind the bar and is always incredibly sweet, offered to fix my dreadlocks. We had a party on the beach, and I danced all night till a beautiful dawn came. During the last sunset, which was lovely, pink and dramatic after the rain, as soon as I thought it was a perfect day for dolphins, they appeared, at least seven in pairs and groups of three, they stayed in the bay for a long time, and even jumped the highest

I've seen. Beautiful slick black silhouettes against the pink and cobalt blue sea.

Yesterday morning, I caught the ferry as the sun came up: the water was as still as a lake, everything was pink. I got to the main land and, two bus rides later, I reached El Cuyo. Unfortunately, I had slept the whole of the first leg as I was tired. I was awake though, when we approached El Cuyo. Driving over the bridge that crosses the lagoon, there were hundreds of flamingos on either side. What a spectacle.

One sleepy square with the church, a few tiendas and a few dusty roads running along the coast, or perpendicularly to it, towards the lagoon. Just like I knew I would, I love this place. The beach is wide, very long and virgin, the sea is not shallow for ages. There are a few palapas you can sit under for shade, the plants are tropical, there are palm trees and the lovely sound of wind running through their leaves everywhere. I found myself a room close to the beach in the main square where an old lady runs the place.

When I go and check out the beach I am also overjoyed by the lack of mosquitoes and chakistes(midges) There are a few biting ants, but that's nothing. A stroll around the place and I really like it. I love how long and wide the beach is, with all the palm trees and lovely houses on the beach front. They are obviously for rent now, but I like that they are all quite small and look nice. There are no big buildings or big hotels here, no trendy bars on the beach, then there is "nothing "more. Just virgin beach. The vegetation around streets and houses is also stunning, all the slightly bigger properties are tastefully disguised behind lovely foliage. Suddenly, I meet an American guy called Cody, who invites me to drink on the beach with his mates, Lorena from Mexico, Rudy from Italy and Cody's girlfriend, Stella, also from Italy. Cody has been travelling for 7 years, he's always doing something and has tons of energy. He fishes for food, builds fires on the beach to cook or picks coconuts off the trees to eat and he's incredibly resourceful. He also arrived here only today, but somehow, he's already able to organise a house for me. (I love my room on the beach, but can't cook there, and there are lots of lovely houses here with gardens).

09.10.21

Yesterday I slept in my new house. It has a lovely patio with a garden all around it with large palm trees. The bedroom has three windows and there is a large front room/kitchen with windows and doors everywhere. Everything is a bit smashed up as this is Mattia's holiday home. He has never rented it before, so it is just as it was left by him last time he came here, with things like garden furniture, for example, in the lounge. I just moved some stuff I needed, brushed the floor, hung a hammock on the patio, put a sheet on the pillow-less mattress (luckily, I am very happy sleeping without one) and the house is perfect.

I also bumped into a few people that I knew from Holbox, Tony and Bruna, who came here with Rami so now we are all hanging out together. They have friends living here, people they met in the past, either here or in Holbox. We spent a lovely night at Costa Coco, the house where they live with some cute puppies and kittens, sharing lovely food and another night we had pizza at a very nice place run by Argentinians (hence the food was great, including the ice cream)

All these people living in El Cuyo are incredibly laid back, I could see myself living here, I think. There are also lots of cute cats, lovely bird sounds and general ambience. I am told there is a croc at the fisherman pier, but I am yet to go there to see it.

There is a palapa built on stilts above the lagoon where people go and do yoga in the morning, and they are not pretentious, perhaps I should join them tomorrow.

Perhaps I should come here to spend the whole of the last month of my trip in Mexico in March. I've already seen dolphins on two occasions, and they came really close to the shore.

12.10.21

I've just arrived in Cartagena, Colombia and it sounds just like Naples with mopeds, dogs barking, traffic and beeping. I'm in a bit of a shock after all this time away from big cities. As the buses and planes were freezing, I also wore shoes, socks, long trousers, and a sweatshirt for the first time in ages. The coaches are so cold, and with tinted windows, the landscape outside is muted and dulled down; you start thinking it's winter and that that's the real temperature. Then you get off, the heat hits you and the vibrant colours come back to the scene. What can I say, I left Mexico after 6 months! and a crazy, last few days at El Cuyo, which I really loved. I got to play music and enjoy my patio, although I didn't get around to draw the view through the house gate, which is a shame.

It has been full of extremes, such as lunching with a rockstar and half the town in the morning, and dining on the same day with Stella and Cody in a tiny comedor, basically someone's house, run by a mad mama with the weirdest inflection in the voice that reminded me of the crazy guy in Police Academy, and her daughter and friend. We ended up sharing beers and a cake with the family, as it was the daughter's birthday. We suggested they get a candle for the cake, and they picked up a normal fat church candle from somewhere, completely dirty with bits stuck to it and plonked it right in the middle of the cake. The cake was nice, but I didn't eat the edge close to where the candle had stood. What a crazy night, impossible to describe...

I've really enjoyed hanging out with Tony and Bruna, who I knew from Holbox but hadn't had opportunity to really chat to, so we got to know each other a lot more. We also got to hang out in one of the best houses on the beach, which was lovely, with its garden and big palm trees being on the beach itself. Rami has been very kind and charming to all, and was making sure I felt included, as did everyone else.

Yesterday afternoon, I left my guitar with Bruna, who should go back to Holbox, and I took the bus to Cancun. I slept at the station whilst charging my phone, comfortably on the metal chairs in the semi deserted bus station. I could stretch out and lie down on three seats, luckily. At 4:00 a.m. I left for the Airport. After the usual stress and tribulation of getting a million online forms filled on a dying phone, I've managed to board my plane. At this point, I only had three spliffs left of the ones I rolled for the journey and the first day in Cartagena, therefore I walked through customs very relaxed. All the flights went smoothly, only two dogs at Medellin, but they didn't look like drug dogs. The dog came close as I was asking a question to another attendant but I didn't mind at all. When I got to Cartagena, I caught a taxi, and with the driver went to buy some pot before going to my accommodation, so that was quick! I knew he was ripping me off, I even told him, but I was sleep deprived, not thinking straight and too eager to sort the weed out.

21.10.21

A lot has happened in the last ten days. I've visited Cartagena, which, as I mentioned before, has a soundscape like Naples, with the mopeds and horns. Many people look Caribbean, which I didn't expect. The historical centre is cute and pristine, with lovely wooden balconies and flowers all over the place, the old city walls speak of pirates and tropical storms and look out over the large bay and huge beach. Outside the old town, I was hit by the poverty, people rummaging through piles of rubbish, sleeping in the streets. I was glad my hostel was in this part of town, just across from the lagoon, so that I got to see this reality.

The guys at the hostel were cool, so I stayed one more night in order to explore Cartagena a bit more. I walked along the city walls and went to the modern art museum (wow, a bit of culture). I strolled about, talked to some people, bought another tiny guitar, visited a few parks, and had to bribe a young policeman, who caught me rolling a joint in one. The hustle and bustle, the people, all the stuff in the supermarkets, returning to civilisation was a complete shock to the point that, as I was waiting to cross the road at a traffic light, I had this clear realisation that it is actually madness to be living in such crowded places, where we need a system of traffic lights to cross the roads and get about.

Last Friday, I left for Palomino, a small town north of Cartagena, on the Caribbean coast. A public bus took me to the coach station, and 8 hrs later I arrived in the dark. I got to my accommodation, and it wasn't until morning that I had a chance to appreciate where I was.

The town is squashed between the sea and the Sierra Nevada, its beginning just beside us, indigenous people live here. They dress in immaculate white clothes, large hats, most are tiny. The town is encompassed by large trees, bananas, willows, palms, tropical forest.

The place I am staying at, Aldea, has a lovely garden which keeps cool in the hot hours. Everyone at the campsite is friendly. There are Andrea and Seb, who are young parents to 15 years old Michelangelo, and work with offcuts of leather making beautiful things. They are trying to make a life out here. They arrived last week. There's Natalia and two-year old Joel, there's Santiago the volunteer and Muñeco, an old musician from Brazil. I spend three lovely days here, I sleep in a hammock for two of those nights, it's really comfy, and once you have the mosquito net around the hammock, nothing can get in. I tried my new guitar, and I am pleasantly surprised, as it has larger frets than the old one, more like a normal size guitar.

Something amazing happened at the campsite. One rainy day I went to play some guitar under the palapa whilst the others were cooking and eating. At some point Muñeco returned to chill out in his hammock and I didn't stop playing, I mean, I did, but he told me to start again and, I actually did! So, the campsite was being very good to me, but it's rainy season and everything here is so cheap that I started looking for private accommodation. I put an ad in the Palomino Facebook group and lots of people got in touch. It was fun to explore town, going to see all these rooms and houses. I even got to go up into in the mountain, past a crazy house made of corrugated iron with sculptures coming out of it, what a mad place.

I almost rented a little house on the first floor of Juana, a lovely lady with a huge pig in the backyard. A spiral staircase goes up to the landing above her house. In front of you, a wooden plank acts as a bridge to the toilet and bucket shower, to the right, a little door opens on the "kitchen", an open area with a gas camping stove, and a small room, with a single bed. I go to see it twice, she's even put plants outside, a hammock and a table on the other roof, where normally she hangs her washing to dry. It's perfect for me, overlooking the smashed-up path, children playing below, the house nestled in the trees, with a lovely view of the Sierra Nevada. But then, on the day I am meant to pick a property, one more comes up, round the corner, and it is one that Juana manages. So, she shows it to me, it has a room, a garden, two outside palapas, one with three hammocks, one with the kitchen, it also has a van converted into a bedroom at the back of the garden. Of course, I love it, and I'm going to be sleeping in the van. Normally this property would house many people, but since it is low season, the landlord decided to give it to me dirt cheap. Impossible to say no. So now I live with a rooster that wakes me up every day, and at night sleeps amongst the crockery, and five tortoises. They are gorgeous, with specs of white on the face and red on their elephant looking legs. Their shells are intricate, I've seen three so far. The big one came out to say hallo and bit my big toe. Oh, by the way, my toenail is back.

I haven't been going out at night yet, mainly because the weather is a bit moody at the moment.

22.10.21

This morning I woke up and was stunned. Actually, for the first time, I saw the Sierra Nevada, usually hidden behind thick cloud or haze. It's like the Alps, the peaks are high and covered in snow. Whilst down here, it is boiling hot. The mountain that I can see all the time, which I thought was the Sierra, is a very small mountain in comparison. It was almost like a dream, because five minutes later, it was gone again behind the clouds, and I have not seen it since.

The beach at Palomino is great, and feels ancient with various trees, and tall palm trees going right to the water's edge. The sand reminds me of Citara beach in Ischia, where I spent my childhood summers, and the sea too, as here it's not very shallow. it also has waves, it doesn't look like the Caribbean sea, at least these days. Two rivers end up in the sea at either side of the beach and, since there has been a lot of rain, they have been carrying leaves and debris, making the water close to the shore murky. They also make it nice and cool.   I met Maria form Bogota, who came up to chat to me, and told me of the life of the indigenous people in the mountains, now I want to go and explore. The days are getting shorter quickly, so I think I'll do it in the morning. I don't want to be still up there when it gets dark.

The road down to the beach is lovely and peaceful too, shaded by huge trees with massive roots. I love walking here. Iguanas have been replaced by large lizards with a purplish hue in the green skin.

There are no tortillas here, but Arepas, which are flat corn discs, but they are a lot thicker and whiter than a tortilla and get cut in half like a bun, and then filled with whatever, meat or cheese, very tasty!!!

I'm loving the yucca too! I had it in a wonderful soup. There's a lot more plantain being eaten here and slightly more vegetarian food in the comedores, so I am having a bit more fun, going to eat out in non-tourist places, ...and, you can buy smooth pasta shapes in the shops!

Mosquito bites are one round pinprick, not the two triangles, shaped just like a vampire bite, like teeth, that you get in Holbox. You can hear the storms and see electric storms before the rain comes; before the lightning strikes, and thunder passes over your head, shaking the ground. Strobe clouds, powerful thunder, bright flashes, then big dollops of rain, making a thin white curtain, everything is so dramatic out here, when you are always outside.

23.10.21

I didn't go to the beach, instead I went up into the mountain looking for indigenous communities. I saw a few people coming down, with a horse or maybe a mule, a pointy hat, dressed in white cotton, mainly women and children. But then I took a wrong turning, and I ended up by the river, not up in the mountain, so, I'll have to go again. The trees were huge, the river wide and not too fast. A lovely walk, with that little bit of fear of the unknown.

Why does going to the woods makes me feel slightly melancholic? It's happened this morning, just like it did in the Laguna del Tigre, in Guatemala. All that energy, but maybe also because walking in the forest (tropical or not) reminds me of the UK, it makes me slightly homesick, introspective, and reflective.

On the way back I bumped into Seb and Andrea. They were going to buy weed, so I decided to tag along, meet the dealers and buy some while I was at it with whatever money I had on me at the time. We walked through the house, into the backyard, where three guys were selling anything you want amongst the chickens. Well, at least weed, regular or "creepy", and coke. The guys were friendly and I bought two bags. If I stay here longer, I will be able to go without my friends to buy weed. I'm in two minds about staying. The mosquitoes have been pretty bad, and I've been too lazy to go out at night, so I've just been sitting in the garden, and I have been eaten alive. I'm going to make an effort tonight, despite the weather, to go out, I'll make my mind up after this.

25.10.21

Some of the shacks outside where I live, are only made of four wooden sticks and tarpaulin all around them. Some kids play at throwing coins against the wall all day long (which for days sounded like someone clipping nails with a nail clipper, and I couldn't understand how it was humanly possible to be at it all day!)

The rooster is not so scared of me now, especially after I fed him a couple of times, the pasta and lentils went down really well, so did the raisins. Now he actually comes close. I am starting to get slightly attached, it makes me think of Comi the cat, who I left behind when I "closed" the campsite in Holbox, I hope she's okay.

I'm so happy I have been able to connect to people back in Europe with the power of Wi-Fi on the mainland! I even managed to do Pilates and yoga classes on line with my regular teachers which has been great.

26.10.21

I stumbled upon an after party on the beach yesterday afternoon and of course, I joined in. I had a great time; people were really cool. The waves were crashing, the sunset, then the black sea and a huge orange halfmoon. I like that most people I meet here are Colombian, although they may be here on holiday from other places, and the party was no different. I got on especially well with two brothers and their friend. Pepe, Natalia and I didn't get the name of the other brother, but he said to me he's been partying for six days straight, he said to me "Marina, these feet, do you know how much they walked? they walked to Rome, of pure dancing!" They were so sweet, they reminded me of my friends and I growing up, we would always be the last to leave the dancefloor when the party would finally close. That's why we clicked, I think, they could see that in me. They offered me some drugs, but I didn't take them as I had never heard of them, so in the end, around midnight, I did leave, although the party was still in full swing. They may still be there now, who knows.

28.10.21

I went up in the Sierra, exploring. I followed the very steep path to the top, where I could see Palomino below, and the ocean. Here, the trees are massive. I met a few Indios coming down, it wasn't clear if they were happy for me to go up, I met

some kids coming back from school; imagine having to go up this steep dirt road every day for school. It was very peaceful though, not a piece of litter in sight. When the path started going down again, it seemed to go on forever, so I decided to return the way I came.

MY VAN - PURA VIDA

I have been making friends with the tortoises this morning. One of them loved the raisins, the other hated them, and actually likes poo! The one that loved them, allowed me to gently stroke her head, we are friends now. They are so funny and full of personality, and memories of my little terrapins and the childhood house in Vomero, flooded in, but you know, I have a soft spot for turtles. They were even showering this morning (there is a leaking pipe, sprouting a nice jet of water, which they use to shower) so cute!

With the rain new flowers come out all the time. New banana leaves shoot up looking like massive spliffs as they start to unroll into the big majestic leaf.

30.10.21

The other night I was bitten by a dog. Nothing too serious luckily, just one more wound on my smashed-up legs. Yesterday it didn't rain all day, and in the evening, as I got to the bar I started hanging out at, it started to really piss down for hours. That meant we couldn't go to the party on the mountain as the path would be too flooded to get there. I had been looking forward to it. The bar I am frequenting is actually a corner shop, selling everything, including drinks. Outside, it has wooden planks as tables and tree stumps as seats under the portico that runs around the shop, it is a great hangout free from rain. The shop even has a toilet a couple of doors down the portico. I started to think it's the best bar in the world! The people hanging out at this bar are very cool and chatty. A lot of Colombian and Venezuelans. They made me feel welcome straight away, and everyone has been very respectful and laid-back, so I've been feeling really good there. All the Venezuelan people I am meeting, men, women, and children seem very nice, it makes me want to go to visit their country.

I came home last night, in the pouring rain, after the failed mountain party, only to find a party with good music right next door. I didn't gate crush this party, but I enjoyed the music from the van, before falling asleep lulled by techno music. I have been considering the sound design here. I live close to all these families, it's like a giant campsite, with almost none of the properties made out of any significant material. Apart from the house of the resident DJ, which is also the only house that seems equipped with all mod cons, things like furniture. They even have a generator for power cuts. Maybe they are drug dealers, who knows. All the other properties are wooden, or made of breezeblocks, or just tarpaulin; you hear TVs, radios, chats, chickens and birds, washing machine all at once. Inside, the shacks are very barren, maybe just one single space.

31.10.21

My neighbour is not a drug dealer, it's actually a collective of DJs called the Bogotá project or something along those lines. Hendrix the surfer told me.

Last night there were parties all around me in Palomino. (I felt incredibly sleepy after pigging out big time on a veggie burger, my eyes were shutting, so I had to go home and sleep) and didn't join any of them. A cacophony of sound, faraway electronic, Spanish songs closer, all blasting through the night. (At least here there's not too much Cumbia and Reggaeton, it's more Spanish songs, so I guess it's better. At least I can amuse myself translating the cheesy tunes.) Anyway, I suddenly, in the middle of the night, woke up to the sound of the van door being open. Obviously, I shouted in Spanish "what are you doing here" and this man just said" I've got the wrong house" and he scuffled back the way he came (which was over the fence). How can you say "I thought it was my house", you wouldn't climb over the wall into your own house. Anyway, I never even saw him, it was almost like a dream. Then I went back to bed lulled by the unlikely music mix, and I probably would've doubted it had happened at all, but in the morning, I did find one of the outside sinks had come off the wall, which is probably where he had come in from, damaging it.

06.11.21

I left Palomino behind, with sadness. I really liked it, what was great about it, was the mix of locals, many interesting people in their thirties to fifties live there. On my last night there I went to a reggae gig with Hendrix, the surfing instructor who was always very kind to me, and a French couple who were also very nice.

Next morning, after a nice walk by the river and the beach, I boarded the coach to Taganga, a small fishing village close to Santa Marta, the oldest Spanish settlement in Colombia.

I catch a moto-taxi to Taganga from the market in Santa Marta. It's evening as we ride down the bendy coastal road, the driver stops at the viewpoints and shows me the city of Santa Marta below us first, then, after a few more bends, Taganga on the other side of the mountain. Nice of him giving me the tour, and it feels just like getting to Minori on the Amalfi coast, a series of bends revealing breath-taking panoramas at every turn, to then arrive at the town, that spreads out from the main road up into the mountain on one side, and the promenade, with the beach and small fishing harbour in the bay, on the other side.

Their buses are also blue, just like the ones on the Amalfi Coast. I wonder if in high season the road to town gets as busy as the one in Italy. Taganga is quite scruffy and a little edgy, people seem to readily break bottles and brandish them if they want to fight. I'm in Colombia now, there's loads of cocaine, maybe that's a contributing factor. But the vibe is definitely different from Palomino.

I find an ok room overlooking the bay. Living here there is young Vladimir, an American-Russian, who has been here for months as he's doing a diving course. There is Liz who runs the hostel, she is young, and has a young daughter with her. There are others that come and go, and everyone is really laid-back. The place is a bit scruffy, but it's okay. There are three adorable kittens, two are Vladimir's, the other adopts me. I am calling him Shitster as he apparently likes to mark his territory; a fact I am yet to verify first hand, thankfully. The mosquitoes here are super small and flutter about, and almost make no noise, but they're still bloody annoying, and everywhere, especially in my room which has no mosquito nets. I end up closing the window and having a fan on, which is a great system. I don't mind closing the windows as they're very big, and with the fan on it is fresh in here, it feels as if the windows are open when I look out and see the trees waving around in the wind. My room is right in the trees, which is lovely, and I have a little balcony.

In the evenings I go for sunset by the beach and sit on the wall, sometimes sipping a beer or chatting to random people who usually suggest and describe other locations so I discover where I'm going to go next. I spend my birthday like this; I am stoked to notice it's the first time I've spent my birthday in swimming trunks and in the heat!

One day I go and visit Santa Martha, which I liked as it's an older, scruffy, even more real version of Cartagena. I don't know why I was shocked about it, but I was not expecting it to be buzzing with people and shops in the more modern part. I wander about, wondering "why do we need all this stuff?" The shops are full to the brim with everything you can think of, mostly useless stuff, which I'm finding just ridiculous, just like the feeling I had at the traffic lights in Cartagena. I don't know, after all this time in places where all you can get is basics, when I'm confronted with city life, the whole thing just feels crazy.

In Santa Marta I also bump into a Christmas shop, which in the heat is just weird, and into Muñeko from the Aldea in Palomino, who is playing the piano in the cute touristic alleyway with all the nice restaurants, where I get a lovely coffee ice cream. I am stuffing myself with all sorts of crap this week as my periods have stopped and I am trying to gain some weight. When I return to Taganga, I go for a drink to my "next best bar in the world." Again, it's a shop with everything and a bakery with tables outside, on the sea front and, important detail, a toilet. What more can you ask for? Maybe that they lower the volume of the distorting speakers blasting out reggaeton? That, yes, you could ask for, but of course you don't as it's part of the charm. I wonder whether Eros Ramazzotti, the Italian singer, who seems to be very famous in Latin America, has done any Reggaeton collaborations. I keep thinking he has the perfect voice for it already. I like watching the sketchy life of Taganga from here. Various men come to offer me drugs or invite me to their place for some fun and somehow can't quite believe it when I decline, which cracks me up; you should see the state of these suitors! Yes, the vibe is definitely different here. In the daytime the promenade is filled with cheap, delicious restaurants serving what looks like amazing fish. On the beach, on the right-hand side of the bay, on wooden stalls, the fishermen display and sell their amazing catch, I see some huge fish and lobsters. They still fish here with traditional methods. Some boats are beached for repairs, and I love the huge pelicans perched on them, I enjoy looking at them while I have breakfast at one of those places on the seafront. Obviously, and unfortunately, the town beach is not particularly clean but there are others dotted around the bay, so I explore a few, which is nice as you have to walk up the indigenous trail over the mountain. This whole experience feels particularly homely, as it feels so much like the Amalfi Coast, even the sea and the small beaches resemble the Med.

10.11.21

I have enjoyed Taganga and my crazy neighbours who all of a sudden would take some coke and go wild for a while. You can buy very small bags of coke, hits really, just like you can buy loose rice, pasta, flour or beans, coffee or shampoo sachets, loose eggs, seeds, raisins and nuts in Colombia, so people can "afford" to get high, and they do; any time of day, any day.

After eight days I left Taganga behind, and took a coach to the mountains, to Minka, a small town on the river, perched amongst lush forest, overlooking Santa Marta below. The whole thing still feels like the Amalfi Coast, going up to Ravello perhaps, but with a Caribbean look about it. There are loads of funky birds and trees, huge butterflies and insects here. The place I'm staying at, Dunarinka, has great views and it's very peaceful. Last night, going to the toilet I saw a snake. I arrived in the evening and soon after it was dark, so I went into town. Three barking, scary dogs live really close to the house; well, since I got bitten, dogs are a bit scary. I decided to carry a stick on my way back, but luckily, they were not there. There is a cute little white church in the town and not much else, but right there, in the square, I straight away bumped into the people I met in Taganga who suggested I came here. They were hanging out with friends and learning dance routines. We spent a nice couple of hours hanging out. This morning I explored more, I went to Las Piedras, where two rivers meet and walked about the steep roads looking at the lovely plants and birds around me. At dusk the colourful birds get really vocal and have crazy chirrups. I hope to see a toucan.

DUNARINKA 11.11.21

I went to Pozo Azul this morning. A beautiful one hour walk on the road cutting into the jungle (the first part is for cars too, the second half is a path) huge bamboo trees, metres high, the sticks larger than the size of my thigh. It was a nice fresh morning to walk uphill hugging the river below. At times, great sound design. Then I arrived to Pozo Azul, where there is a pool below a small waterfall before the river speeds up again into rapids.

12.11.21

I went for another stunning one hour walk to the waterfalls of Maneka, and an icy dip in the water that literally took my breath away. On the way back I met one of the town dogs whom I am calling Orb as he has one eye only. He decided to go back with me (he was almost at the waterfalls, really far from town) so we walked together, waiting on each other at different points. It was very sweet. Once we got to town, he quickly got distracted by other dogs and left me.

I saw three toucans. Here, they are small birds, but quite colourful and with a large beak (considering the size of their bodies) they are Caribbean toucans.

Last night I went to a party in a bar and met a few people and danced for a few hours to some weird, crazy tunes and at some point, an insect bigger than my hand, decided to join the party and rested on the wall for at least an hour.

13.11.21

I love walking in Minka, getting out of my house to go to the town, I just love it. Today I decided to go to Los Pinos, a three hour walk up into the mountains to see the view from up there. What a walk, tiring of course, but the birds and the nature all around it were definitely worth it. Coming back down, a man directed me to a shortcut, and I went steeply down the mountain, through someone's coffee farm, deep into the forest. At times the paths were so thin I got scared I was following a path originally made by water rather than footfall. It was a bit scary when I wasn't sure where I was going, looking around at the huge forest, no mobile signal, and already very tired as by this point, I had walked almost non-stop, mostly uphill for five hours. It takes a lot of effort to calm the mind in this situation, but you have to, and cool and calmly, have to keep going, otherwise it's worse; you can't give into panic or desperation, but I could see how, if I didn't hold my nerve, my imagination would start thinking of all the scariest scenarios. Of course, it wasn't that bad, as I could hear the river, so sooner or later I would get somewhere, but being already tired, I didn't want to get lost, or go down a path from which it would be very hard coming back up. Luckily, I met two people going the opposite way in one of these points where I wasn't sure where I was, and they confirmed I was on the right path. In the coffee farm, I also had a vision of what this would be like if I were actually walking through some cartel's coca farm or something. These mountains were not safe from criminals until recently. Luckily, they are now, and I had an amazing walk.

18.11.21

I left Minka on Monday morning; after a journey of probably eight hours involving a few bus changes and a motor taxi ride, I got to Rincon Del mar. The journey was slightly stressful because at every change people were bullshitting me, or overcharging me. I had one guy selling me a ticket telling me the bus was direct to Cartagena. Instead, after many stops, I even had to change bus in another town before getting to my destination. Alarm bells had rang when I saw that the destination on the front of the bus said Barranquilla, but by that point the guy I had paid was nowhere to be seen. On another leg, a guy tried to overcharge me, but I protested and he quickly backed down. Another guy, knowing I wanted to go to Rincon Delmar, without me asking -actually I had asked him not to- arranged for a tuk-tuk to come and get me to go to Rincón. I had to walk off and went to the moto taxi area where a guy offered to take me. We started down the unpaved road and after a while he stopped close to other people. I asked what was going on and he said he had to wait for a better bike as his one didn't have headlights. I was tired, so I did complain to him that he shouldn't have accepted the job if he knew his bike was not up to it, that I only wanted to get to my destination and I was tired of people bullshitting me all day. So, he actually started to drive but I asked him "didn't you say we need lights? " "yes" he replied, so we stopped again. Luckily the better bike arrived soon after, we switched and off we went, huge mosquitoes splattering in our faces, the sky pink with sunset. Emanuel and I chatted a bit on the bumpy way, he was actually cool.

Not until the next morning I was able to have a good look around the small beach town, with virgin beach either side, rickety wooden bridges, lagoon and the simple, unpaved central square with wooden benches in the sand, shaded by trees. The sea is lovely. I got a hostel where the dorm is in the huge roof and my bed overlooks the bay, stunning.

I love walking on the beach in the morning, and just dip in the sea before coming back to the hostel to prepare a nice breakfast and eat it on the hostel's tables on the beach, looking at the sea. I'd like to stay here till the end of my Colombian trip, if I find weed. In this town they don't really like potheads, or so it seems, so people hide to smoke and I'm yet to meet the local smokers. The hostel is empty apart from Ivan, the Italian volunteer looking after it, so the vibe is quite chilled. I don't think I have seen more than ten tourists. The town feels quite busy with locals, there are many men of all ages which is strange. Actually, there are people of all ages, which is weird because in towns like these, usually the twenty- to forty-year-olds seem not to exist as they usually move to cities for work or something like that. People here look definitely Caribbean and their skin has a beautiful tone. They are a noisy bunch though, even for Colombian standards, I would say.

On another note, the mosquito bites, which seemed to be more or less confined to the leg part, here spread up my thighs with perfectly round bloody holes (once I've scratched them).

RINCON DEL MAR 18/11/21

On my walks I have seen a maths or chemistry class, I couldn't quite tell, (sorry mum, I should know!), in the street on the side of the road, I saw a man building a canoe on the beach with an axe using some driftwood he found, a huge crab pinched my big toe in the house and it made me jump because at first, in the corner of my eye, I thought it was a large scorpion (it was whitish)

19/11/21

At the eleventh hour, I finally met Sergio, the local dealer and scored some very expensive pot, at least it's not bad pot. I can relax about it now and really enjoy the next 10 days. I've already been told off by my neighbour for smoking too close to her children.

21.11.21

One of the local masseurs, Aleda, asked me to teach her and her daughter a yoga class, so the other day, at sunset we did it and it was fun, although challenging to give it in Spanish! then they invited me for lunch at their house to thank me. It was nice to visit one of the local homes, which of course was very basic, meet the other daughter and all the people that popped by in that hour. We may do one more class before I leave.

I've been left alone at the hostel with Alvaro the humongous nightwatchman as Ivan, the volunteer, left. Since then, the kids have taken over the hostel and they're so cute but completely wild. They are only four or five years old and very loud, so I've also had to engage with them a bit which has been fun, break up fights and calm the mayhem. One day I was doing yoga online with my teacher and a few of them sat down alongside me to do it for a few minutes and it was really sweet.

CP.09.149 BARRACUDA

Today I'm nursing a massive hangover after spending the evening drinking Aguardiente, made from sugar cane, with Sergio, until he tried to get a bit too close, so I went to bed.

24.11.21

I am doing loads of swimming, walking, reading, playing guitar, writing, drawing and thinking. I have read a very nice but also sad book called "the end of your life book club". I've taken to sitting in the sandy Main Square in the evening, just after sunset as it's fresh there and there are less mosquitoes. There is a billiard room across the road, and I've been enjoying watching what goes on in there, making up stories in my mind and generally watching the life of the square. Usually someone ends up chatting to me which is nice and I'm getting tiny glimpses of the life of Rincon del Mar.

Suddenly

I get images,

Of small details,

Of insignificant,

Little habits.

Which we shared

1 million years ago

Drinking a milky coffee in a large white China cup

-A thing we haven't done in years-

It made me think of France every time.

And I can almost taste

the digestive biscuits and

all too quickly

see our old flat with no floors in Peckham

Oh, everything was so new to me then!

How different we were.

And I have to push the images away.

As fast as I can

Because it hurts

And painting floorboards

has never felt

this painful,

this lonely

25.11.21

I absolutely love my bed facing the sea in the huge open dormitory.

Today I woke up to a beautiful day, went for a great walk and a couple of swims and realised that probably yesterday I was in such a strange pensive mood, mainly due to the stormy weather, and a bit because I just finished that sombre book. Incredible how much the weather affects my mood. It's probably why in Palomino I was feeling so uneasy at times.

26.11.21

There was a huge storm in the middle of the night, with chunky rain and strong squally winds that in the end, I had to move to a different bed as rain was flying in from all directions, and I was starting to get wet. I picked up my sheets and chose the bed at the far end; luckily, I had the choice of ten.

27.11.21

So, it finally happened. I was robbed. In the hostel. Fortunately, they only took the money that was in my rucksack. No bank cards or documents were stolen. I believe it was a guy who just showed up yesterday, but how could I prove it. They sent him away anyway and later showed me a picture from two years ago of a "criminal" who had come to town, and it looked very much like him.

30.11.21

I'm leaving Columbia today, right now I'm at the airport. It was a stressful journey as the coach was very late arriving in San Onofre, but luckily, I'd left enough time. Although I wasted an hour even before starting the journey, I got here on time.

I had a lovely moto-taxi ride through Cartagena. I do like the new town, a mix of tin rooved shacks, lots of art deco, and I do like the one or two storey houses with high iron gates, and the tarmac roads and pavements so distinctive of the Americas.

I am going back to Mexico, to Holbox, but first I'm going to hook up with my old friend Sannette, who I haven't seen for at least four years as she lives in the USA now. We're going to do some cultural sightseeing before going to Holbox in a couple of days. I'm really looking forward to seeing her.

15.12.21

Finally, I am back in Holbox and my beloved camping Balam! It's been an intense couple of weeks. First, I arrived in Cancun late at night after a whole day travelling, shared a cab into town with a German girl coming to Mexico to do some spiritual retreat, and made my way to the hotel Sannette had booked. She was already asleep, so I stayed out in the hostel's garden in the fresh air for a while before going in. In the morning, we had a brief catch up over breakfast. We also met Iria from Tribu, for she was in town. She helped us find the car hire place and then we went off to Chichen Itza to see the ruins. We stayed in a lovely hotel close to the archaeological site and the next day we went to visit it with our guide Louis, who was very knowledgeable. The pyramids were great, there is one, where, if you clap your hands in front of the stairs, the sound gets amplified, and it sounds like the bird quetzal! That was very cool.

Then we went to swim in a cenote, a sink hole filled with freshwater and whole ecosystems, of which there are many here in Mexico. Whilst we were there, Sannette realised that doing this was on her bucket list! It was nice to be able to cross it off together so unexpectedly. We went to visit Valladolid, a cute little town with a lovely central square, and then we made it back to Cancun with two minutes to spare, to catch the shuttle bus into Chiquila. We were giving ourselves twenty minutes, but we took a couple of wrong turns in Cancun, and suddenly we were going to be late. Sannette's quick reflexes and decision-making meant that she was able to make quick U-turns and with teamwork, coolness (and by putting everyone else under pressure to do things quickly) we got there just on time by catching a taxi from the hiring place to the coach station.

We arrived on the island of Holbox at night, at the posh hotel Sannette had booked and we were greeted by a waiter handing us a drink. How sophisticated! The hotel was very nice, with lovely gardens, pool and areas to lounge about on the beach and in the gardens. Sannette and I had a lovely time chatting, swimming, walking and going dancing together. We realised we had never done the latter together before, in all those years in London. We also went on the tour of the three islands which was actually cool, we saw the crocodile that lives there, and we also got to see dolphins. Actually, Sannette was the one who spot them! The weather and the sea were amazing for the whole week and we both had a great time. In the evening, on most days I would leave Sannette alone and go to work. I had an amazing reception from everyone on the island on my return, especially from the people at work, which has been lovely. We had a nice week of music with new musicians. Some of the good old ones and some of the nice old volunteers are slowly coming back too, which feels great. This time around it really feels like I'm a local, and it's been nice to be able to share this VIP treatment with Sannette. Seeing the Holbox night sky on the first night when we arrived felt amazing, and seeing Sannette, slowly relaxing and getting into the groove after almost 2 years cooped up in the house due to Covid, was priceless.

Once she left, I was of course homeless, but Maya, the hostel manager, offered me her house as she was going to Tulum for the night, she has a lovely house. In the meantime, I spoke to Vicky at the campsite, which was still closed after the rainy season. She agreed to let me stay in exchange of three hours of work a day helping to reopen the campsite, so I spent the last four days putting tents up, raking the garden and painting floorboards, which I loved. I am very grateful because I know Vicky only gave me pleasurable tasks to do! Now, we are ready, the campsite opens officially today, and I can finally have the mornings to myself, as this week was crazy.

Everything in Holbox is familiar, but it's slightly askew, it is "definitely" winter. The water is slightly chilly, but very delicious, the sun sets on the left-hand side, the tides are bigger, the days are shorter, and there is sometimes a slight chill in the air. Sometimes I'm wearing long sleeves at night. It's an absolutely gorgeous temperature, and there are less mosquitoes. It's also getting busy, and unfortunately, there is still construction work going on at all the hotels around the campsite. So, I am also looking for somewhere else to stay, which probably I won't find, as it's hard to find anything decent on the island or with no building work quite close, but I'm actually going to look at a few options. I saw a couple in town, but so far Balam is still the best. How nice to see the campsite gradually coming back to life, to rake new life out of the paths. When I arrived we still had no electricity or running water, and, as Vicky gave me the best, easiest, most mediative jobs to do, images and emotions have been flowing freely. I got a bit nostalgic when gardening, collecting the yellowed "Autumn" leaves. I guess it's because I associate all things green and related activities with the UK. Painting floorboards felt so lonely, reminding me of past houses and DIY projects. But it was lovely to be there with all the images and thoughts, old and new, as the campsite regained form. So nice to catch up with Vicky and Lio and meeting the new volunteers.

Oops, the first two guests of the season just walked through the door, sweaty and heavy with backpacks!

20.12.21

I am loving Holbox and the campsite up and running, people of all kinds come and go, and I feel really at home. They have also stopped construction at almost all the sites, so it's going to be quiet over the festive season. Going to work the other day I spotted dolphins, which reminded me, how cool it is, to be able to see dolphins on your way to work.

We've had some really nice music, cool bands, and jams and people are still happy with my work, which is nice. Rami of Foo Fighters has played a couple of times, and of course, when he comes, the atmosphere is electric. Last night after work, some of us went to the beach with instruments and a girl was swinging around this colour changing LED light bulbs attached to the end of a rope, making shapes over the water in the full moon, beautiful to watch.

23.12.21

Alan came back to the campsite and is volunteering, so Balam is again filled with his infectious laugh.

Mati the drummer/volunteer also came back, with British Jake, who was also here in the summer, and Jack, a friend of Jake's who just arrived from the UK. They have a band, so the campsite is filling up with musicians. I miss the nights by the fire looking at the stars. Now I can only do that on Tuesday, my day off.

The temperature dropped a bit more. Everyone, including me, has a cold. Since yesterday, going to the beach reminds me of going to the beach at Easter in Italy, although the sea here is still warmer than the Med in April. I have not swum for the last

three days due to the cold, but Alan gave me a paracetamol and straight away I felt a lot better. Until then, I was concerned it was Covid, since there seems to be quite a lot of it on the island at the moment... hopefully I'll be alright. It is a busy week at work, and I don't want to miss it due to illness. How strange, this will be my first Christmas working like a fool and in the heat! I am sure it will be lots of fun.

24.12.21

Last night we had a great open mic, Jack played the harmonica, a good addition, we don't often get. On my way home, the tide was exceptionally high. I got to the section where there is a low wall and when the tide is high, usually I walk over the wall. At the end of this wall, I lower myself using a stone that's lodged in the sand as a step, then step to the left of it on hard sand. But last night the water was so high that when I stepped to the left, the water was knee-high, the sand, very soft, gave way under my foot and I fell face down in the water with my phone in my hand, as I was using the torch app to see where I was going. I quickly lifted the phone up and, half soaked, I rapidly covered the remaining distance to the campsite, trying desperately to switch off the phone, but I could not swipe to switch off because the screen and my hands were so wet. When I got to the campsite Jack and Jake helped me with this and put the phone in rice. It's still there now, and I'm going to wait a few more hours before switching it on and hopefully, be able to ring the family as it's Christmas Eve.

Today the campsite is super full and we are organising pizza night, Balam style. I am over the moon because I've discovered last night that I don't have to work tonight, so I'll be able to attend!

It's a lovely fresh day; last night I slept with a thin blanket, for the first time! I'm still feeling a bit strange, but I may just be tired so I'm not going to swim, although the sea looked amazing today. I took the opportunity to do some yoga on the beach, yesterday at my "private" beach, and this morning with Jack, Jake and Deyan, one of the new guests of the campsite, I believe he said he's from Germany with Albanian roots. The class actually set me up nicely for the morning, although it was a very different experience: half hour stretches and yoga poses, half hour of breathing exercises. Hopefully I can keep up the routine, inspired by them, who I think are going to do it every day. Better than starting the day smoking!

25/12/21

My phone didn't switch back on, so I was only able to send a couple of hurried texts home for Christmas which sucked a little. Last night we had a lovely pizza party. We made twenty pizzas on the parrilla, the Argentinian version of a barbecue.

Matty made the bases, Vicky and Grazia cooked the veg, we all assembled them together, Alan brought the veg, and others bought the drinks. Then we spent all night playing and singing around the lovely fire of Balam camping. It was the biggest fire we ever made, and it was beautiful and warming up the chilly night. It was a funny Christmas though, more like a regular summer party for no particular reason than a traditional family occasion. Although I guess, we're almost like family here at Balam, some of us have lived together on and off for six months so it's only fair we spent this day all together like a family, and it was lovely.

26.12.21

The colour of the water is incredible today, almost fluorescent yellow, and dark blue, green, grey in the stormy morning. I was very happy to have taken a gamble and gone for a walk despite the threatening sky. Indeed, it didn't rain and now it's actually sunny. The water was fresh, but not cold. Nonetheless, I'm still not swimming this week. I don't want to catch colds and panic on whether it's Covid or not, as there is a lot of it around and Bruna at work tested positive, The vibe at work is basically that they're not going to really prevent suspected cases from going in to work, and they're not enforcing testing. So basically, they're not following any kind of protocol. Morally I've been struggling, the other day when I had a cold, I didn't want to get tested for fear of testing positive and getting stuck at home. If I were in Europe, I would have accepted much more having to test and, quarantine. But here, in the open air, on a tiny island, it feels like we're getting away with it, maybe we're just burying our heads in the sand and finding excuses. I do think though, that at work we could be more careful, and I tried to have a few conversations about it with the managers, but the view seems to be that we can't stop living, and this is their answer to any argument you put forward, so much so that the conversation starts to feel weird, like you're losing your mind and are talking to an automated being living in a different reality altogether. When this happens it stuns me, I start doubting myself and my sanity, like I am under a spell. I get like that when confronted with people who are so convinced of something which is the complete opposite to what I believe.

29.12.21

A friend of GG DJ, Jordan from Canada, who I didn't even know until two days ago, turned up at work calling my name, introduced himself and lent me a phone! Unknown to me, Gigi had asked him to lend it to me knowing he had a spare phone knocking about. How nice of him, and the phone is actually better than mine, which is still in rice. So, I'll be able to stay in touch while I patiently wait to see if my phone comes back to life after a week or two of drying. I was moved by Jordan's gesture. I was finally able to call home for Christmas.

This morning I went for a walk by the beach to Punta Coco, a route I don't often take, my usual route being blocked by two guard dogs. These are both very fluffy and cute looking dogs, but unfortunately, as you approach, they stand on either side of the path like stone statues at an entrance gate and start barking. I just don't fancy walking in between them, especially since the dog bite in Colombia. I was looking down at the ground, to see where I was stepping since I had no shoes, so I didn't see them right away. At some point I raised my gaze, and they were both there staring at me attentively. So, I chucked a right and headed for the beach that way. The water was lovely, fresh and bright blue, I turned left towards Punta Coco with my feet splashing in the shallows and just where the land bends smoothly but sharply towards Punta Coco, I bumped into three huge starfish. One the size of a football! They were yellow with either red dots or stripes along the edges. I picked one up with both hands, it was surprisingly heavy, maybe 300-500 g, the shell was unexpectedly hard. I took a quick look at the alienish underside and gently put it back where it was. I had never seen a starfish that size before.

04.01.22

How nice to spend New Year's Eve in a small town where one lives in the heat. I worked until 3:30 a.m., we had a band then GG DJ, with Mati on drums, he played really well. Then we all went to Salma, a club on the beach. They set up the speakers outside as well as in, so we danced on the beach under millions of stars with more space (Salma is a very narrow and long club). It was nice to just bump into loads of people I knew without having organised anything. I never had such a stress-free New Year's Eve. I bopped to electronic music until I liked the DJ, then went home in the extremely dark night. I missed the dawn by half hour at the most. On New Year's Day, I didn't feel rough, and it was a splendid day. The beach and the sea were marvellous.

The tides are extreme at the moment. In the last few mornings, it's been really far out, creating watery lunarscapes in the bright white sand. Loads of different wading birds have been hanging out, making it really magical.

Last night, as I laid in bed, a huge storm came, and once I found that my tent was holding up, the big dollops of rain lulled me into sleep, not before the tent was wildly shaken by wind and beat by the palm leaves above it. This morning is awfully blustery. My walk to Punta Coco was made squiggly due to puddles, I had long trousers on and didn't fancy getting them wet by walking through them. Finally, my route got me onto the beach, the wind was incredible, the sea "rough" (as the Caribbean can try and be) the colour green, blue, and foamy white but with a certain metallic greyness about it. I stood in the strong but warm wind, facing the sea, getting a bit nostalgic as it reminded me of a blustery day at a British beach, of which I had many: The palm trees disappeared in my mind to give way to images of Welsh Christmas walks, belly-full with food and booze, big coats, scarves and hats on. Although my surroundings looked nothing like it of course, I started to think about that Christmas when we went to, I think it was Amroth beach, and it was so misty and foggy you could hardly tell you were on a beach, everything around us was white, like we were shrouded in smoke, we couldn't see very far at all and could only hear the sea. It was like walking in a dream.

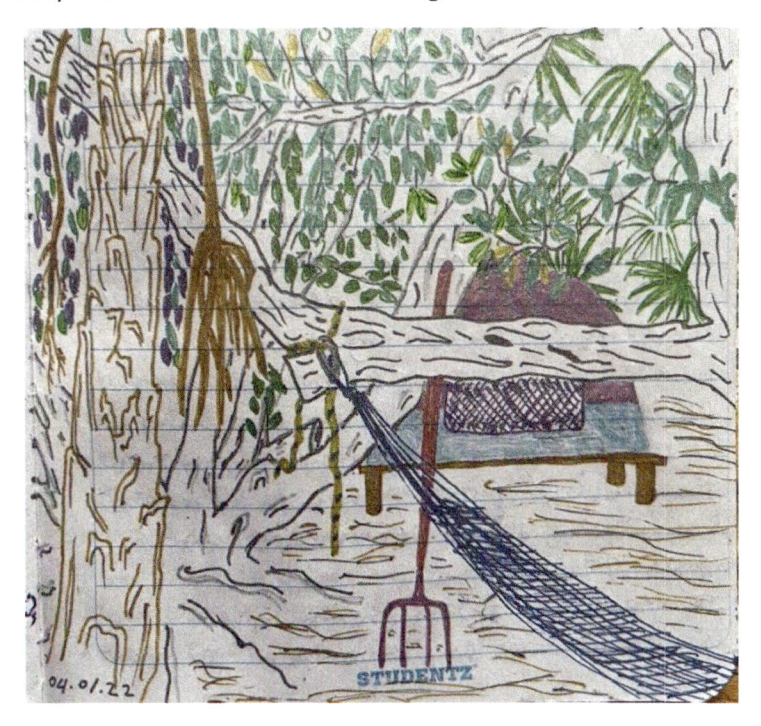

04.01.22 - BALAM

06.01.22

I have enjoyed meeting the people that have come and gone from the campsite, and it's nice to see the core group slowly swelling with a few new plan-less people that are getting enchanted by this place and getting stuck here. They're all very

like-minded people and seamlessly slotted into the daily life of the campsite, adding to the general laid back vibe, well-being and happiness. We all get on very well and connect at different times.

The other night we made gnocchi, directed by Grazia. We made an industrial quantity; we even made some pesto flavoured ones which were green, and some with beetroot, looking a gorgeous purple. They were very tasty, and it was so much fun doing it all together on the huge table of the Balam kitchen. It was funny also because all of a sudden, a couple of check-ins arrived and Vicky had to attend to them with floury hands, other guests would arrive and just watch or take a picture of what was going on, as it was a sight to behold. Grazia also made me a bracelet, which I'm now wearing around my ankle. Then I went to bed and it was so cold that I woke up in the middle of the night. Since then, I'm not too well, yesterday was worse but today too I don't feel 100%

07.01.22

I woke up just before 9 am today, super late really, I went to Punta Coco and did some yoga. I was feeling a lot better, my muscles were not aching. The sea was so inviting that although I had no swimsuit, on my way back, I got naked and went for a swim.

On my walks, the thought of April approaching is coming more and more to the surface. Grazia and her boyfriend Dan, and even Alan are leaving in the next few days. Maybe this is partly why I'm starting to think about it. April is just under three months away, and I'm telling myself that I'll have to catch the plane, that I am looking forward to stay in England for a bit and that it would be nice to see family and friends, but I can't picture what kind of life I'll be living, or for how long. It's a very strange feeling, and I am worried I will not want to catch that plane, although I don't just want to stay here forever. I don't know. Sometimes I feel that in April I'll be ready to leave, sometimes I feel I won't… but it feels crazy that, in just a couple of weeks, I'll have to give notice at work if I want to leave it at the end of February in order to have "one last month" travelling around before going home.

08.01.22

Spanish Marco, Grazia and Dan left today, which was a shame as we've had a great time with them. Carol from Costa Rica and her boyfriend Simon from Germany will take their place volunteering.

On my walks I've been wondering "where did all the crabs go?" You would see the floor moving with them as you stepped through the mangrove just a few months ago, and now nothing, not a single one.

When I made it to Punta Coco for some yoga this morning there were two birds I've never seen before wading in the shallow, they were white ibis, (My dad later told me what they were, he googled it). As I meet birds on my walks, I try not to get too close, as I can appreciate what a great effort it must be to take flight, and I don't want to scare them into flying away.

10.01.22

Nicola, an old friend from college, came to Holbox with his husband Artu, who I hadn't met before. It was nice to see Nico after such a long time. We briefly met, five years ago in Berlin, where he lives. The last time before that, was when we finished college, thirty years ago. The power of social media meant that we were able to hook up.

Just an hour ago, Alan left. This time, as people from the core group of guests leave, it feels more definite: the Holbox era is drawing to a close. Probably none of us, once we manage to get off the island this time, is going to come back here soon. It may even be for the last time. Who knows where and when and if I'm ever going to see Alan again. He's off to Guatemala now, then he may choose to go and study in Europe. In that case, our paths may cross once more.

Last night, my walk home was one of the darkest. The sky was moonless, dotted with stars, everything around me was black. It was a little scary and beautiful at the same time, and I didn't want to switch on my phone torch but wanted to be totally engulfed by the darkness.

Yesterday was emotional; I had many thoughts, guilt, worry, nostalgia, all wrapped in one, a real pendulum lacerating my heart. Thankfully today I'm feeling a lot better.

11.01.22

I just love to find myself in a murmuration of birds, and this morning at Punta Coco that's exactly what happened. As I was doing yoga, about 50 birds swooped beside me. I could hear the air being moved; the energy of such moments is immense. I managed to feel how it must be for a bird, rapidly slicing through air in formation, moving tightly as one, high up, twisting, and disappearing momentarily in the light, then reappearing, sometimes white, sometimes black, tumbling and stretching through the sky like a sheet hung to dry in the breeze, then shooting down and skimming the water at high-speed, wind through the feathers, straight wings. There were three groups flying fast, sometimes close sometimes far away, it was beautiful. I stopped my yoga and just sat there looking at them, until they flew away, and I could not see them anymore.

14.01.22

The beach is always different, every morning the landscape is shifting somewhat, and it makes every walk a special one. Some days the tide is extremely high, some mornings brown seaweed has been washed up on the beach creating new banks, some other day the sea is out for miles, leaving pools of water in the white sand, reflecting small cut-outs of sky. Some days I have to change my route if the puddles are too big, or I just don't fancy going through them.

The other day I noticed that the eagle nest on top of the electric line was alive with chicks, and the two adult eagles were flying and communicating high above, listening to their screeches was quite exciting.

16.01.22

A very strong north wind is blowing, the sea is stormy and swollen, it has eaten away most of the beach. I went for a shortish walk dictated by puddles and tides. The wind was shaking the palm trees, their rustling sound, the low swoosh of warmish wind, the salty sprays of the sea water on the face.

Birds were perched on the wooden poles of the old pier that emerge from the water, gripping against the wind with webbed feet or claws, getting splashed on at times by a bigger wave. I wonder if they enjoy it or if they just withstand it. It doesn't look like a lot of fun, but perhaps it is, because otherwise why don't they fly elsewhere?

I was woken up by heavy rain in the night, and had to close the outside cover as water was getting in. Now I'm trying to dry my shoes in time for this evening. They were left outside my tent. I've been wearing shoes for the last couple of evenings as the floor gets cold at night and my sandals snapped the other day. The phone says the temperature this week is between 18 and 23°, in the evening I've been happy to wear up to three layers.

I almost forgot; the other day a friend's dog head-butted me, now I'm walking around with a scratch on my nose. What's more painful is the actual bump, it feels tender over my eye and left side of my nose. I didn't even notice the blood at the time but Maya, the hostel manager who was looking after this dog, really freaked out about it.

17.01.22

I managed to reach Punta Coco without stepping in puddles. It's incredible how birds, and other animals, camouflage; sometimes you walk right by them without seeing them. The tiny brown speckled birds that scour the beach, almost disappear when they walk through the bedding of weeds that get washed up on the shore. The white crane, almost as tall as me, but so thin and brilliant white, that, at times, it's actually very hard to see against the sea and sand; and it can stand impossibly still, even in moving water.

Last night something funny happened. I was leaving Tribu and bumped into Jake and Jack, so we walked home together. We took the beach as far as it was possible. When we got to the point of turning into the road, Jake was going to continue by the beach so I said, "Hey let's go this way, there's too much water over there." Right at that moment I stepped in a huge puddle, and did three steps before even realising what was happening, the water was calf high, how we laughed. There was a bright moon completely covered by clouds, giving the sky such a colour that it felt like it was 3 p.m. Like a short winter day in London when the sky is about to go dark at dusk.

BALAM-GARDEN

22.01.22

There was a huge scorpion in the kitchen this morning. Nicole, an old American hippie who has been here a week and has been living in Mexico for many years saw it first. Lio unfortunately had to kill it by dropping a slab of wood on it and cutting it in half. The poor scorpion was still wriggling.

I am very slow today. I woke up at 10:30, it's never happened before. Probably I slept in because it was cloudy and fresh. It rained a lot yesterday, and to kill some time, as I was waiting for it to stop to go home after the gig, I asked Preto to make me two cocktails. They were very nice. Can't remember the name, but it was a drink from the 20s with whiskey. It made me think of my grandma, although I never saw her drink any cocktails or whiskey. I woke up this morning, and I can't remember how I got home. I want to know which way I chose and whether I actually walked through any puddles, but I can't remember. I must be hungover...

26.01.22

As I was wading through the shallow water, which was lovely and fresh, I stumbled upon quite a large white crane perched on a defensive wall made of rocks. I was able to pass really quite close without it flying away, these birds are large and not easily scared. I particularly noticed the black clawed feet as they were as big as my hand.

I've taken to going to a different beach lately, close to the beach club Carolinda. Here, the remanence of old piers, wooden stumps come out of the water and are used by all sorts of birds to stand on. There are some funny white birds here, with unkept tufts of feathers on their heads where the ears should be, and they remind me of Robin Williams the comedian, simply because his penguin character in the movie Happy Feet looked a bit like them.

PLANTS DETAIL

22.01.22

There was a huge scorpion in the kitchen this morning. Nicole, an old American hippie who has been here a week and has been living in Mexico for many years saw it first. Lio unfortunately had to kill it by dropping a slab of wood on it and cutting it in half. The poor scorpion was still wriggling.

I am very slow today. I woke up at 10:30, it's never happened before. Probably I slept in because it was cloudy and fresh. It rained a lot yesterday, and to kill some time, as I was waiting for it to stop to go home after the gig, I asked Preto to make me two cocktails. They were very nice. Can't remember the name, but it was a drink from the 20s with whiskey. It made me think of my grandma, although I never saw her drink any cocktails or whiskey. I woke up this morning, and I can't remember how I got home. I want to know which way I chose and whether I actually walked through any puddles, but I can't remember. I must be hungover…

26.01.22

As I was wading through the shallow water, which was lovely and fresh, I stumbled upon quite a large white crane perched on a defensive wall made of rocks. I was able to pass really quite close without it flying away, these birds are large and not easily scared. I particularly noticed the black clawed feet as they were as big as my hand.

I've taken to going to a different beach lately, close to the beach club Carolinda. Here, the remanence of old piers, wooden stumps come out of the water and are used by all sorts of birds to stand on. There are some funny white birds here, with unkept tufts of feathers on their heads where the ears should be, and they remind me of Robin Williams the comedian, simply because his penguin character in the movie Happy Feet looked a bit like them.

PLANTS DETAIL 2

30/01/22

Juan Rama, the Colombian rapper who sings in Jake and Matt's band, "Sleepy Jake, and the Cooking Monsters", organises the cleaning of the Mangrove in a kayak once a month. Today, they were actually cleaning Punta Coco without kayaks, and they were building rubbish bins and painting signs, so I had no excuse really, I went along to collect rubbish. There was not too much of it, main offenders seemed to be ladies' underwear and cigarettes butts.

31.01.22

I've taken to checking the BBC website every now and then just to try and make Europe a more concrete thought, and not just this far away concept, completely alien. Sadly, it seems to be working.

I do feel like I'm ready to go to Europe to see family and friends, I know this much. Beyond that, I'm not sure. I'm scared that, after a painful adjustment I will just slot into the usual life, and I don't think I want to. I'd like to stay in Europe a few months and use it as a springboard for future trips. But I am petrified I'll just get sucked in. I should not think of it now, it's still so far away and only in my head. I should concentrate my energies into researching my last leg of the trip and get off this island. Friday, I have a meeting with the boss to give my notice in. It's getting close, it's getting very real.

02.02.22

On my day off I was able to catch a glorious sunset at the campsite's local beach. As I was sitting there on the rocks watching the sky change colour a million times, the realization that in three weeks I should really leave Holbox, hit me hard and that suddenly felt incredibly soon. I feel so unprepared, and I think that in three weeks time I won't feel like leaving Holbox at all, and I will have to force myself to start travelling again. And yet, on the other hand, I also feel excited to start thinking about moving on. It's just, three weeks seems an awfully short time to get organised, especially as I have no idea where to go. It would be good to start researching. Of course, I have the faintest idea where to go next, but it's very faint.

Today I was grateful for all the people I have met here, I've learnt so much from them on so many levels, from cookery, to language, to myself. I don't think anyone knows how grateful I am for this. I've learnt so much from Vicky, Lio, Matty, Jake, Jack, Gabby, Simon and Carol, Alan, Grazia and Danny, and the list I'm sure is longer.

05/05/22 - LEAF

06/02/22

I bought some Jasmine incense, so I'm thinking of Nonna Linda a lot, she loved the smell. I had a meeting with Davide, my boss, to give him my notice, he asked me to stay till the 25th of March for the anniversary of Tribu, 12 years, I don't know what to do. I have a few days to think about it. He also asked me to stay or to come back in September, very nice of him, but I doubt I'll ever be back once I leave. It's good to know though that for now I have an open opportunity. But I should not be lazy and come back here because it's easy and have connections, although life here is pretty sweet. The balance between work and life is just great really, so why leave? Why look for it somewhere else? I tell myself that Holbox is getting too busy, and I'm really to find the "next new place". But for the time being, my quality of life is just amazing, so I do question why quit when it's still so good.

08.02.22

The flamingos are back! One flew over my head as I was doing a side plank. I just knew I'd see one. The light and colours were amazing: Greys and blues and then the pink flamingo with the long spindly legs. I was so happy to see it.

11.02.22

I gave my notice in. My mind is split and in overload, I can't even begin to write about it. Because of all this confusion and inner turmoil, I'm glad I'm taking the last month off to really think about it or, better still, to feel it!

14.02.22

−14.02.22 LEAVES

15.02.22

15.02.22 - BALAM

19.02.22

This week Sleepy Jake and the cooking monsters left the island to go on tour busking around Mexico. So nice to see them go on this adventure. I'm sure they're going to have the best of times! So, there has been a switch at the campsite, all the musicians have gone, now we are full of artisans, as a few people making necklaces and other stuff have arrived, more or less at the same time. I'm going to miss the boys, it was very nice to live amongst them and to witness their creative process. I realised it's something I missed. I am now totally aware that making music and generally being creative is something I like, and I need.

Anyway, something amazing did happen. The other day I was playing in my tent when Jack went to his tent and ended up hearing me play a song. He started asking me to hear it again. Two or three days later I actually played it in front of him in the afternoon. We were sitting by the fire circle and as I was playing, also Matty and Jake came back from the beach, so I ended up playing in front of all of them. In front of very accomplished musicians, I was less nervous than I thought I would be. But of course, now they're gone, who knows if I can hang onto that feeling and keep opening up and start seeking musicians to share music with.

Meanwhile in Holbox, the sunsets are now slowly moving back to the right, towards the centre of the island and we are starting to lose the shade that we had gained in the previous months as the sun is higher in the sky. At night the moon has been full and bright, lighting my way. Two nights ago, Iria from Tribu gave me a small amount of magic mushroom so I was a little high when I walked home in the night. The sound of the sea was amazing: I seemed to be able to hear in incredible detail every little ripple, every little wave, every fizzing bubble. Everything looked slightly different, the sand under my feet was pixelated. I felt so peaceful and happy, and the high felt very natural and healthy. I had had my reservation about doing mind bending drugs on this first trip alone, but this experience was extremely nice, chilled and mild so I felt very safe, and I was just in a really nice mood.

26.02.22

I saw the biggest starfish, it was bigger than a football, probably thirty centimetres across. Dolphins are also back. I was watching one epic sunset last night and just as I said, "all we need now is dolphins," I saw a fin coming up very close to shore, and silhouetted against the huge orange setting sun, which was just touching the water, a small puff of cloud looking like a mountain right in the middle of it. Then a few more dolphins appeared, and swam there for a while, what a sunset.

The other day, on a completely different note, another crazy thing happened, after soundcheck I actually picked up the guitar and sang a verse of one of my songs as the other guys were setting up the bar. Everyone stopped what they were doing when they noticed, I then stopped. But that was a start, I guess. I know I shouldn't have stopped, that's the first rule, isn't it? And I let myself down, but I'm not going to beat myself up about it. I guess I'm slowly improving as lately, a few people have stumbled upon me when I am playing on the beach, so they kind of know about it. Also, I've been playing in my tent at times when there are others around, as the urge of doing it sometime has been stronger than the urge to hide. Also, I realised that this is a very safe place to try, probably the best, as everyone is incredibly encouraging and supportive, and therefore I've been thinking, if I'm ever to do it, I should not lose this opportunity. Maybe I should play with someone, someone like Elsa, as I feel very relaxed around her, or play the whole song after sound check, as the bar staff wants to hear more, or on the beach, or by the fire at Balam. All this craziness is clearly a reaction to my impending departure. I feel completely "alla deriva" at the moment, adrift, like a dead starfish being tossed about in the tiny waves. I am just following the current, brain frozen on automatic pilot. I guess that's the price I will have to pay if I'm not able to make a decision or commit to something. If I can't make my mind up, I will have to catch that plane. I understand it's always me really, putting myself in this situation. Because all of this year was improvised, there's a feeling of it being temporary, a finality I can't quite shake off. Unless the next three weeks travelling bring about an epiphany, I think the best thing will be to go back to Europe to see how I feel about everything by closing this circle. But then sometimes I think, why bother? Why do I need to do it now? Why do I need to know? Then again, with the Visa running out and my British phone not working, it might just be easier to go to Europe, organise everything again, and then move on, as right now, bureaucracy at home, in London is starting to slip away and from here it's difficult to sort anything out.

01.03.22

One month to go... Oh God! I keep telling myself that this island is truly on the way to being ruined by progress, and that this is a good time to call it quits. In the last week more wooden structures and sun loungers have sprung up on Punta Coco; almost every day I notice new building work as I walk to the beach. Lately, as I do yoga in the morning, sometimes I hear construction noise not far away. In the little microcosmos that is Holbox, the other day I had a total awareness of what we are losing, as every day my quest for tranquillity brings me further and further away, but the island is so small that soon there will be nowhere left to go to find peace. I had the strongest, clearest emotion, I felt like a wild animal losing its home, I kept thinking of the footage I saw once of a monkey in the Amazon standing on a tree fighting the diggers that had come to destroy its home. Here in Holbox, as the change is so tangible, I had a moment of total clarity and identification with that poor monkey, even more than when I first saw the footage, this time I felt it. I was outraged, surrounded and powerless. The inevitability of it almost choked me, it felt like there was no air to breathe and I struggled to collect myself.

On a happier note, it's been carnival all week, with loads of partying in the main square till the early hours. Yesterday, I went with Lio and Vicky to see the final parade, where the carts with the musicians, the dancers dressed in sparkly sequin dresses, and big colourful plumes of feathers, were performing and singing. After half an hour of arriving, Vicky suddenly fainted. It was worrying, we took a golfcart taxi home. Tomorrow she'll go for tests, what a strange episode, hopefully it's nothing serious.

05.03.22

Last two days of work, tomorrow the last jam night, I think it's going to be really good. I am getting ready to party. For the last two days I've been training the new sound guy Alex, also called the Cayman. He is a 24-year-old Mexican from Cancun with various tattoos, even on his face, including a Cayman. He tells me he used to box professionally, that's why he has that nickname.

I am glad I'm going to stop working but I'm also going to miss it. I had a great time at Tribu where I've been constantly shown so much love from everyone, it's insane. I still can't put into words how I feel about getting so close to the end of this trip; for weeks now, it's been an emotional rollercoaster. At times I get sudden images of my house or London, or, when I'm lucky, it's the British countryside and coastline. How long will I be able to hack it in the city? Should I move somewhere rural? The only good thing about going back and confronting the old life, is that I will be forced to understand what kind of life I want to live now.

11.03.22

My last night at Tribu was great. All the musicians came to play and show me their love, it was so emotional, they dedicated songs to me. Martha even sang in Italian! Then on Tuesday I got a bit jealous of Cayman as he was smiling away all night, and I thought I handed him the best job on the island. I went to Cabo Catoce with the rest of the staff as we have been presented a tour by management. Cabo Catoce is wild, untouched and lovely. Unfortunately, I was there for a short time as most of the trip was spent fishing for a Chevice lunch. Obviously, I didn't particularly enjoy this part, but it was also interesting as the bait was big chunks of fish, not tiny worms, and the fish the guys were catching were huge. They stayed the night there, which must've been immense as there were loads of shooting stars and bioluminescence in the sea. We also had a last pizza night at the campsite, music around the fire and in the kitchen with Nick from Colorado and other passing musicians. So yesterday, finally, with a heavy heart, I left Holbox not knowing if I'll ever be back but knowing I have a home there, at least for a while.

Now I am in Merida, I arrived last night, and I have to say the city is lovely. A Spanish looking city, plazas with trees and ample seating. It reminds me of a modernised version of Antigua Guatemala. Here the buildings are a liberty style, and all the facades are painted in bright colours. The historical centre is very clean, there are free music and other events. On Paseo Sixty, the main tourist road, I found many modern art galleries, so I spent the morning visiting them. What a great day, I had been starved of visual art. My favourite piece was a suspended blanket made of used teabags, the art work was called "Duermete" with a play on words of the "te" which means tea. I also really liked the work from a Spanish artist who grabs bits of city walls, and makes new paintings out of them. This project was right up my street!

14.03.22 RIA CELESTUN

17.03.22

Two hours away by coach from Merida, lies the sleepy fishing village of Celestun. I arrived here on Sunday late afternoon and, when I got to the campsite, was overwhelmed by the crappy Reggaeton blaring out of the restaurant speakers, in the otherwise super tranquil settings, and I thought I got this wrong, I couldn't stay here. The beach was also quite crowded with families. Luckily for me, since then it's been quiet, and the restaurant has been closed so all I've been hearing all day, is the loud blackbirds with the crazy chirp who live in the palm trees above my head.

I like that feeling of letting go and accepting that I need to adapt, to enjoy a place which, on first impression, was not to my liking, I was resisting. I am in love with this place now; my tent is right on the beach under a canopy of palm trees. Although I've been sleeping on the floor -for some reason the landlady will not give me a mattress, she said they were all punctured but I don't believe her- I have been sleeping really well. The beach is very wide, the sea blue and it's really peaceful and relaxing, especially after the madness which after all, is Holbox. Anyway, this is a proper holiday now; in Holbox, because of work, I seemed to experience the beach differently: most beach walks were made to go someplace, not just wander and explore. I've been able to really relax here, and get into playing guitar, drawing, and writing. This is why it's nice to take my time in places, if I travel too quickly, I don't have time to jot it all down.

The moon was full last night and I woke up right on time, early this morning to see it set into the water in front of me, all big and orange at first, then taking this strange dream like opaque shade.

Another cool thing that happened unexpectedly: I went on a boat tour, which I really enjoyed as it was very informative. As part of the tour, we visited a rain water hole where flamingos hang around. Here they naturally harvest salt when the pond is dry. Sergio the guide said the saline pond was very good to cure fungus and other foot infections. I have been struggling for two months now with a nasty infection I've picked up in Columbia and no cream seems to really make things much better. When Sergio said this, I put my feet in the water at once, for maybe five minutes top. I didn't think much of it and indeed suspected it may make things actually worse. But no shit, I woke up the next day, no itching, and no burning sensation since! It's been two days now, I'm over the moon! Fingers crossed it doesn't flare up again.

18.03.22

I love sleeping here in the generous garden of Ria Celestun, shaded by the tall palm trees, their long leaves rustling in the deliciously gentle wind, creating amazing patterns of shade and light everywhere, repeating in muted tones hundreds of natural shapes. The birds constantly calling and flying around, sometimes stealing my food.

There are also three lovely dogs here that are always happy to see me and want cuddles, which is nice, and sometimes we go for walks on the beach or watch the sunset together.

Armando and his wife look after this place and are really nice, just like everyone in town. Everyone is very relaxed and friendly. Nice to be in Yucatán, there is a nice vibe, nice to finally be in Mexico! And getting to know people and customs. Here the foreign tourism is very sparse and until now they seem to have catered mainly for Mexican holidaymakers.

The town itself has a main square with a tree-lined, benched Plaza of course, including a lovely red church with a woman in the courtyard that rings the bell by pulling at a rope, there is a yellow clocktower with an arch, a few restaurants and the basketball court, and an indoor market, where, it's nice to see, all sorts of lovely fresh veg and fruit are available. Oh, how different life on the mainland! as opposed to island life.

There are a few roads running parallel to the square and beside the town, there is a large lagoon with the port and a very healthy number of small, traditional fishing boats. There are also many more of these ponds, lagoons and general bodies of water all around the back of town.

In Celestun there's also a wide cement pier where people fish from, kids dive, couples admire the sunset and pelicans inspect, from a safe distance, the work of the fishermen as they dry their feathers.

On my beach walk there are also other birds, As usual, I cannot identify them, nonetheless I recognise all of them from cartoons like finding Nemo and it entertains me to see them, as I feel like I'm in a Walt Disney picture.

19.03.22

The weather has been absolutely gorgeous, maybe that's why it's so hard to leave Celestun. Here, the pelicans floating on the waveless, pond like water, make me think of British ceramic gravy boats on a shiny blue tablecloth.

Today, on my furthest walk here, hundreds of what I call "tiger fish" because of the irregular patterns that resemble the light reflecting on the water, were swimming in the shallows. I walked all the way to where there were no more houses, just virgin beach; the water was so nice I got completely naked and went for a swim -I didn't have my trunks, when will I learn?!-.

SKY AT CELESTUN

20.03.22

As I was busy drawing, I didn't notice how quickly the campsite was filling up. When I raised my eyes off the page, I was surrounded by large Mexican families, couples, groups of friends. Everyone was Mexican, tents had sprung up everywhere, hammocks had been hung on almost every palm tree available. The wooden tables that are available had been pushed together to create longer ones. The drinks, and different sound systems came out so that when I went to bed around 10:30, amongst all of this, it felt like going to sleep in the middle of three distinct garden parties happening at once. I fell asleep in the end but was woken up around two in the morning by revellers on the pier. At least here it's not always Reggaeton, in fact they also played some club music from Miami, and in general, here they play more mariachi corroncha songs than Reggaeton, which is much nicer, both in musicianship and lyrics.

Anyway, I digress. Last night there was also an epic sunset. Huge and straight in front of us, from the pier it looked even bigger. The sky had gotten dark with thick clouds, so when the sun appeared below them, the colour was incredibly moody.

As the sun disappeared behind the horizon, a dolphin came to fish in the bay. I stood there in the wind to watch it for five minutes, until it went away. Generally, here the sunsets have reminded me of Neapolitan ones, for the dark purply tinge that everything takes after the sun has set, and before it gets completely dark. In Holbox it was a pinker, golden sort of sunset. Yesterday, I was also considering the fact that this year I must have watched over 300 sunsets on the water, how fortunate I have been.

This morning I went for my early walk and, oops I did it again, I was skinny dipping as it was rude not to jump into the perfect water, the beach all to myself, when three dolphins appeared really close, like maximum ten meters away. They were fishing so they were extremely active, twisting, flapping, spraying and jumping in the water. They put on a full show just for me. They were directed towards the town, so I came out of the water, put my clothes on and walked back along the beach, following them and admiring them for the whole time. At some point, they appeared to work in pairs, one was raising almost vertically out of the water to then slap the water with all its weight, I imagine to stun the fish. I saw a fisherman on a boat beating the water with a stick just two days ago, so I wondered, who learned from whom.

Celestun turned out to be pretty magical, in a scruffy, scrappy way. One other great thing about it is, I have noticed many new trees being planted and almost no construction work which is a very welcome difference from everywhere else I have been in Mexico.

Talking to the locals, I discovered there was a bad hurricane here 30 years ago, I think it was called Gilberto. The hurricane was very powerful and destructive, the sea ate away at the beach, considerably, the water level rose, and the mangrove started to die. Now they have a petrified wood that you can visit. It was considered a natural disaster and since, there has been a project of reforestation, the locals are very environmentally aware, and care about trees, and all of nature in a way I haven't seen anywhere else I have visited so far in Mexico. As they explain all this to me, I tell myself that the hurricane, as devastating as it was, was probably a good thing, as it ignited the ecological conscience of this town.

21.03.22

How exciting to be swimming and seeing rows and rows of pelicans skimming the water and coming straight at you, only to form a line once they get too close, and then they zoom past you at eyelevel. Flying crockery. Today I leave Celestun. I've really loved my stay, right down to brushing my teeth! Because I really enjoyed washing at the outside sink and watching the reflection of the tall, curved palms in the mirror.

Funny thing; today the campsite has been taken over by loads of old Mexican bikers in full leather-biking gear.

22.03.22

Just before I left Celestun, I bumped into Alex, a local musician who plays the flute outside the restaurants, I haven't heard him but that's what he said he does. He came to hang out at the campsite to have his packed-lunch and we chatted about music and Mexico, the war in Ukraine and then, when he asked me to play him something, I actually played him two verses of one of my songs, in the campsite, full of bikers.

Later I boarded the full bus to Merida, chatted to the lady next to me and got my bag to stink of fish because I stored it in the cargo area of the coach, where other people were transporting fish from Celestun, amongst other things.

At Merida I caught a night bus to Tenosique; I slept, waking up here and there; a fat moon in the sky, first orange, then white, the dark shapes of trees over an immense flatland, bisected by a dual carriageway. In the morning I was finally woken up by the rising sun, tinting everything with gold. Once arrived at Tenosique, I had intended to sit down, have breakfast, and calmly plan my next move, but when I got there it was a bit too early, and it looked like the bus stop was far away from town. Of course, it actually wasn't, but I didn't know and when I saw a taxi driver outside the coach station, I asked him to take me straight to my hotel. After a very expensive ride of two hours, we realised we had gone to a different place, in the opposite direction to where I was meant to be. So, he decided he would drive me to Palenque where I could join a bus, he didn't want to take me to the hotel anymore as it was too far for him.

Arriving in Palenque, I didn't remember it being a proper town when I was here last time fifteen years ago, but I may be wrong as last time we arrived in the dead of night. All I could remember was a roundabout close to the ruins, with a massive stone statue of an indios face in the middle of it. Although it was still there, now there is a whole town around it, even a bar with a "ten girls on stage at any one time" sign. I boarded a collectivo with a few people, and two crates of chicks, there must've been easily over fifty piled together, and they clucked in the back all the way. I slept on and off to the sound of their loud and incessant cries, every now and then glimpsing at the view, which luckily, was getting more like jungle, so I was hoping to be going in the right direction this time.

The collectivo left me at Saint Javier where a "taxi", a smashed up red car with no numberplate, collected me to enter the Lacandona park.

The place where I am staying is lovely, I splashed out on an expensive room, and I have a patio with a hammock right over the river. All sorts of vegetation, birds and creepy crawlies are about. I went for a thirty-minute path walk around the property, where I have seen some huge trees and learned about them by reading the information placards. Then at dusk, the monkeys in the distance, oh, that familiar sound I missed so much. Being here reminds me a lot of being in El Remate, we're actually very close to Guatemala here.

When night fell, the sky was incredibly busy with stars and loads of fireflies started dancing around, just like in Palenque fifteen years ago.

Apart from having to kill a full family of five amazing looking golden horseflies because unfortunately they were biting me whilst I was playing guitar on the porch, I spent a peaceful afternoon surrounded by huge plants, trees and leaves. Lying in the hammock outside, reminded me of the hammock days in Pankor Island in Malaysia when I was ill and had to spend quite some time resting, and there was a beautiful tree there with lots of gorgeous exotic plants crawling onto it, I used to spend hours looking at it. Tonight, a moth the size of my hand came smashing and thrashing about for a while. Incredible, its wings actually looked like thick autumn leaves.

RIO LACANJA

The selva of Lacandona is inhabited and guarded by the Lacadonan people. They are the guardians of this forest and there are only a few ecotourism places here. They even ask you to take all your rubbish away with you when you leave the area. A few people sell artisan craft: Dream catchers, necklaces made of seeds, and the like; in terms of quality, they are the best ones I've seen during the whole trip. Some men wear a traditional long white tunic and long hair. I went to the centre

of the community, a twenty-minute walk up the road, through tall trees, a few banana fields, cornfields, wooden huts, chickens roaming free, pots on open fires, a couple of places selling dusty packets of cookies, crisps and a few other items of basic necessity, a couple of churches, empty wooden stalls that are maybe weekend eateries.

The river is never too far away, here and there you cross bridges, or get glimpses of small waterfalls and rapids. There are birds with incredibly bright plumage, intricate patterns, and peculiar songs.

At Campamento Rio Lacanja, I have also enjoyed looking at the jungle while I brush my teeth. I've been pleasantly surprised at the relative lack of mosquitoes, although the golden horse fly bites are big round holes on a raised skin bump and there are lots of them.

25.03.22

Since I have been bitten, I have been itching loads, and had two bad nights. Now I remember the constant burning and itching, almost hallucinogenic and heart stopping sensation of the bites in Guatemala in El Ramate!

Apart from that, I went on an archaeological adventure deeper still, into the jungle to Bonampak and Yaxilan.

At Bonampak It's possible to see some frescoes depicting life of the ruler and some huge, carved marble steles, which are very beautiful. It's impressive how they are there, such delicate, thin sheets of marble standing like monoliths in the middle of thick, remote jungle.

After an hour snooping around, a magical sense of peace from the top of the pyramid, over the treetops, eagles flying above, I set off to the next site. A tuk-tuk, a shuttle ride, another tuk-tuk, and a forty-minute boat ride later I got to Yaxilan! Part of the charm of this site is that it lies next to a river. At the river crossing I waited for others to share the price of the boat and thankfully, a Mexican couple arrived, and we decided to split it. We boarded the long, thin, wooden lancha, and we set off across the river; on the other bank, almost at reach, is my beloved Guatemala. I can see families bathing, and washing clothes in the river, as they do. I am so close I can make out the hairstyles and almost feel that Guatemalan vibe, so different from Mexico's. Also, on the river, I see again those super industrious, intrepid flyers, those very tiny little birds that I used to admire on the lake at El Ramate, on the Mon Ami pier. I imagine how, from here, you could possibly, relatively easily, smuggle yourself into Guatemala at the town of Bethel, just ten minutes boat ride on the other side, avoiding border controls.

We get to Yaxilan, they have this way of nestling the long tip of the boats on the sandy bank and push against the current to keep the boat steady without anchoring.

We arrange to meet Murdoch our driver in two-hours, and we separately go and visit the site. Yaxilan is much bigger, with many structures, two Acropolis, and a ball game court. Crucially for me, tall trees coming out of pyramid steps, I've always wanted to see that. Howler monkeys and massive leaves all around, and a beautiful river running next to it. Again, the most amazing thing is the atmosphere, the calm and peace. I really enjoyed it, even the Mexican couple did. They told me when we met again to share another pleasurable boat ride back.

I got home after experiencing life at three dusty crossroads of Chiapas, complete with peacocks and hens roaming free. I took a taxi, sharing the back seat with a ten-year old child, and a friendly, toothless local, who had invited me to share the taxi and I had a chat in the shuttle bus with someone who said amongst other things that last year they met an Antonella Esposito, "from Naples, right?" I asked. "Yes, of course" he replied. "I am also from Naples!" I revealed.

28.03.22

On Leaving Rio Lacanja the next day I got to the crossing to catch the bus to Palenque and when the guards standing there saw my guitar, they asked me to play something. I ended up playing two verses of Canned Heat "I'm on the road again" to two young guards with guns, by the side of the road, a bendy dual carriageway deep in the middle of the jungle, which was frankly, surreal, and a lot of fun, actually.

On the night bus, Palenque to Playa de Carmen, at the checkpoint they almost busted me; I had an empty weed bag in my satchel, and when they searched me, the policewoman found it. I fumbled an excuse of it being my purse, which is true as I have been using these plastic bags to carry money since I lost my wallet all those months ago as they are a little waterproof. Luckily, after a couple of questions, she didn't search me too thoroughly and didn't find the weed that by this point I had concealed in my sweater's sleeve. It's cold on the buses so, luckily, I was wearing a long-sleeved top.

On the coach, I was sitting right at the front, so I had a good view through the cracked windows in front of me, and I was also entertained by the playful team of four drivers, who joked all the way.

I had a few hours to kill in Playa del Carmen. Walking around an urban centre I got the sense that I'm actually in America because of the architecture, street curbs, pavements, urban furniture, and shops. On this trip, because I've been totally immersed in nature most of the time, I have not often thought about the fact that I am in America. Perhaps I thought that I'm in the Caribbean, but it could be almost a beach anywhere, if that makes sense.

Twenty-seven hours later I arrive, guess where? Holbox! For the anniversary of Tribu, and as usual I got an incredibly warm reception. Nice to be able to say one last goodbye to my friends at Tribu, and the campsite too. It's all change! Even Lio and Vicky are off to Costa Rica on Monday, the campsite owners are going to be looking after the place, Scott, who's only been here two months is going to be the one who has been here the longest. It will be another week, another vibe at Balam. Already, in the three weeks I've been away, they have made changes, Scott has been busy with the chainsaw and things are slowly taking a different shape. This time it really is it, tomorrow I'm off to El Cuyo to chill out for the last four days of this mega trip. Oh God! On the plus side, I don't need a PCR test to enter the UK, all restrictions there have been lifted this week, so I will certainly be on the plane... I feel like throwing up. I think I'll go to the beach now...

Holbox is different once again. In these three weeks I've been away more shops have sprung up, but also, being winter, it's now very noticeable that the trees have lost their leaves, which feels crazy, since it is still very hot.

29.03.22

I've left Holbox for the third and, this time it feels a very final, last time. I'm waiting for the last of three connections in a café at the bus stop in Colonia Yucatán. Today I'm really having moments of anxiety, thinking of going back to London. I will go, but I don't really see why. I was talking to dad the other day, he asked me "Are you not bored?". Although from previous instances I believe he uses the word, bored, for lack of a better one when he's very scared about one of my crazy ideas, he made me think about the last year, all I've learned, seen, experienced, smelt, tasted, done. I wonder, how can he ask a question like that, when I've just told him that a few days before I was swimming with dolphins on a deserted beach? I've learnt a new language, new recipes, and customs. I've seen exotic animals and plants in the wild, I've been bitten to fuck by many things, I felt the sun, rain, and wind at all times. I've learnt how to tell the time for the two hours prior to sunset by just using my hands, and I love that. I had a dream job in paradise, I've seen different cities, landscapes, art. I swam almost every day, seen over three hundred glorious sunsets, met incredible people, met all sorts of people. I've started to learn to share things like food and music, which is the most valuable thing that has happened here and I was not expecting, I released baby turtles to the huge oceanic waves, seen a turtle in the wild laying eggs, I've been teaching kids some English, I've been deep into the jungle with a team of biologists, I've learnt of plants and growing food in the jungle. I didn't learn to make a fire, but I have an idea on how it's done. The list goes on as this diary has recorded. So, I don't know how he can ask me if I'm not bored yet.

Anyway, I am directed to El Cuyo for a last three days of quietness, hopefully, and then, whoosh, London here I come, ready or not, here I come. No, not ready.

30.03.22

So nice to be in El Cuyo, I do like this town, although even here, there are a lot more, new holiday apartments being built. Indeed, right outside where I stayed last time, the first two nights they were building, I felt that was probably going to happen. This time around, I had credit in my phone, which meant I could ring any property I fancied from outside, most rentals are clearly advertised with the WhatsApp contacts. I was able to get a nice room, with a huge front lawn, quite quickly. I seemed to be the only one there, I had the very pleasantly ventilated patio that the rooms shared all to myself. I have felt very creative and enjoyed improvising here. Alejandro and his family were also very nice, of course I'm in Yucatán now, where I really like the people.

After securing the room I walked just outside of town, where the road cuts the river and water gushes through wide openings, constructed into the bottom of the road. The tide was low and hundreds of flamingos were feeding and hanging around on a sandbank that formed somewhere in the middle of the river, not far from my viewing point. I watched them for a long while before heading back to dinner. This morning I went to look for accommodation in the wilder side of town. Although, I enjoyed my stay in the spacious room with windows on both sides, I found a campsite where there's no one else staying that's run by three Mexican women of different ages Maria, Margarita, and Angelica, two of them are smaller than me! I loved them and the campsite below the tall palm trees instantly, one block from the beach, so, I've moved here. My tent is a tepee, and I can stand in it. There's a double bed, and I even have a hammock right outside.

31.03.22

I have just been stung on my bum, by a wasp. The ladies gave me ice to put on it, and all is well. I found out that Maria and Margarita are in-laws, as two of each other's sons are married to two of the daughters of the other. I don't know how old they are, but Margarita looks in her sixties.

I slept well in the pyramid tent. I only wish I could remember my dreams. I must be having some crazy ones. It would be nice to see hohow my subconscious is processing the approaching trip.

PAACH KAN

To say that I am freaking out, is putting it mildly. It is absolutely incredible here today; I regret not having come here earlier. Of course, I'm very happy I visited the sites I did in the last three weeks, but the original idea of spending quite some time here, rent one of the cute huts for a while, is highly appealing. I love the look of the place, and London is 2° to 8° degrees today, so it doesn't look like I'm going to manage to escape winter after all. God help me, I don't want to sleep in a room, inside. Where will I go for my morning walk? I love walking on the beach.

01.04.22 Last night I witnessed something that warmed my heart. There was a meeting in the main square basketball court, and the town was out in force to oppose a new development of flats, it was lovely, and vocal, loud, and in the end the developers had to leave without gaining any sympathy whatsoever. "El pueblo unido jamas sera' vencido" they proudly and rightfully shouted at the end. This battle was clearly won! Hopefully the war won't be long, and they will win it.

I don't really feel like ringing anyone today, I don't want to talk about tomorrow, I know that if I really start thinking about it, I won't get on the plane.

02.04.22

So, this is it, the 2nd of April is finally here. Technically there is still time for a Visa run and money to get me to El Remate, Guatemala, but I'll go home. If nothing else, because I can't keep this diary forever, carrying notebooks around the world! I need to close the circle and start a new one. I have some half-baked plans of throwing a few seeds here and there workwise in the UK, see what happens, while I plan my next trip, but boy this is hard, especially because I really love El Cuyo. I love the architecture, the wooden huts, I love that there are a few people handmaking amazing hammocks and ants are big, like one centimetre long. Here, I would be certain to find just the right place, as many of the properties fit the bill. But anyway... Ohoh, this is so tough.

It's been an incredible year, I've learnt so much, seen so much, grown so much, obviously not in a physical term. I've met so many good people, it's been amazing and I'm not going to forget them, some are good friends now.

Realising I was going through a musical journey as well as everything else, was probably the biggest revelation of the whole thing. I hope that I can keep everything I've learned and don't freeze up again, in freezing London... Boy, I am scared. I'm not ready to face reality: I've noticed that TV annoys me, with all those city sounds, and mindless chitchat! Oh, God, I'm either becoming old really quickly, or I realise that sound in general really affects me and shapes my decisions and influences my moods. I like people if I like their voices, or music with specific sounds, and certain soundscapes will be the reason why I visit somewhere or not, that kind of thing. Well, I'm freaking out, I don't know what to do with my little guitar, will they allow it on the airplane? when and where do I leave it? It feels bad, like abandoning a pet on the road...

Well, it's time to put my shoes back on.

Acknowledgement

A massive thank you to Emma Hope-Fitch and Vernon Douglas for proofreading, discussing this book with me and generally encouraging me!

Thank you also to my friends Hugh Griffiths, Cristina Meloro and Tiba Fazeli for supporting me and being close to me even when I was on the other side of the world.

Printed in Great Britain
by Amazon